a world of stone

First published by O'Brien Educational
11 Clare Street, Dublin 2.

ISBN 0 905140 15 X

Cover Design Dan Grace
Book Design Michael O'Brien
Binding John F. Newman Ltd.
Typesetting Redsetter Ltd.
Printed by E. & T. O'Brien Ltd.
11 Clare Street, Dublin 2, Ireland.

a world of stone

941. 708
20 26 71 81

THE O'BRIEN PRESS
11CLARE ST DUBLIN 2

THE CURRICULUM DEVELOPMENT UNIT

The Curriculum Development Unit was established in September 1972. It is sponsored by the City of Dublin Vocational Education Committee and works in co-operation with the School of Education in Trinity College, Dublin, with the approval of the Department of Education. It has a steering committee composed of representatives of these three bodies.

The Unit has concentrated on the curricular areas of Humanities, Science and Outdoor Education. The Unit Director is Anton Trant.

Humanities Co-ordinator:	Tony Crooks
Humanities Team:	Nora Godwin 1973-
	Agnes McMahon 1975-76
	Bernard O'Flaherty 1976-

This collection has been researched and edited by
Paul O'Sullivan
with revisions by Nora Godwin.

Prior to publication, the following schools were involved in the development, use and revision of the collection. The suggestions and comments of the teachers in these schools have been used as a basis for the edition.

Colaiste Dhulaigh, Coolock; Colaiste Eanna, Cabra; Colaiste Eoin, Finglas; Coolmine Community School, Clonsilla; Gonzaga College, Dublin; Liberties Vocational School, Dublin; Scoil Ide, Finglas; Vocational School, Ballyfermot; Vocational School for Boys, Clogher Road; Vocational School, Crumlin Road.

Previous page – The Aran villages occupy sheltered sites on the broad terraces north of the summit of each island. In the background is the gentle slope of a poorly developed limestone scarp. The cluster of buildings pre-dated the roads. The small stone walled fields are hemmed in by areas of bare limestone pavement.

contents

THE EVENING LAND

From Connemara, or the Moher clifftop,
Where the land ends with a sheer drop,
You can see three stepping stones out of Europe.

Anchored like hulls at the dim horizon
Against the winds' and the waves' explosion.

The Aran Islands are all awash.
East coastline's furled in the foam's white sash.
The clouds melt over them like slush.

And on Galway Bay, between shore and shore,
The ferry plunges to Aranmore.

Seamus Heaney

Limestone pavement on Inishmore criss-crossed by fissures due to the dissolving action of rain water. Much of the surface of all three islands consists of these barren pavements.

aran
Discovered

 HE ARAN ISLANDS are a group of windswept grey rock ledges on the Atlantic coast of Ireland. The three main islands are long and low, resembling a group of stranded whales, and together they extend over 25 kilometres in an almost perfectly straight line across the mouth of Galway Bay. The name Aran may have been derived from the Irish word *Ara,* which means a kidney, because of the kidney-like shape of Inishmore. It may equally well have been abbreviated from the Irish expression *Ard-Thuinn,* meaning 'the height above the waves'.

According to legend the islands are the remnants of a rock barrier that once stretched from Galway to Clare, trapping the waters of the present Galway Bay in a gigantic lake. This story has, of course, no basis in fact, but it is worth noting that all three islands are closely related to one another and to the nearby Burren district on the North Clare mainland, in the type and bedding of their rock. The largest of the Aran islands, Inishmore (*Inis Mór* meaning 'the big island') lies nearest to the Galway mainland from which it is separated by the North Sound which is ten kilometres wide. Although this island measures fourteen kilometres by three kilometres at its extremities its total area amounts to little more than thirty one square kilometres. Killeany Bay forms a natural 'waist' to the island lying, as it does within a kilometre of the western cliffs. From there the island rises north westward and achieves its greatest width before descending to the narrow 'neck' at Port Murvey less than a kilometre wide. A second, slightly lower

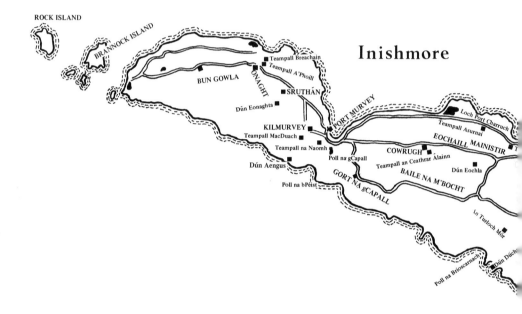

ROCK ISLAND

BRANNOCK ISLAND

Inishmore

Teampall Breachain

Teampall A'Phoill

BUN GOWLA

ONAGHT

■SRUTHÁN

Dún Eonaghta ■

PORT MURVEY

Loch Port Charruch

Teampall Asurnai

EOCHAILL MAINISTIR

KILMURVEY ■

Teampall MacDuach ■

Teampall na Naomh ■

Poll na gCapall

COWRUGH ■

Teampall an Ceathrar Álainn

Dún Eochla ■

Dún Aengus ■

GORT NA gCAPALL

BAILE NA M'BOCHT

Poll na bPéist

An Turloch Mór ■

Poll na Brioscarnach

Dún Dúch

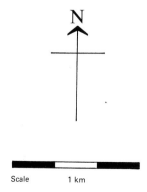

N

Scale   1 km

THE ARAN ISLANDS
County Galway

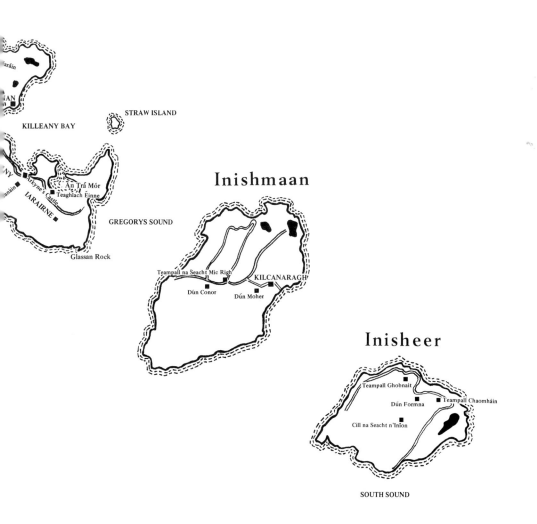

STRAW ISLAND

KILLEANY BAY

Inishmaan

Arkyne's Castle
An Trá Mór
Teaghlach Éinne

IARAIRNE

GREGORYS SOUND

Glassan Rock

Teampall na Seacht Mic Righ
KILCANARAGH
Dún Conor
Dún Moher

Inisheer

Teampall Ghobnait
Dún Formna
Teampall Chaomháin
Cill na Seacht n'Iníon

SOUTH SOUND

The Atlantic breaks over the rocks at Inishmore.

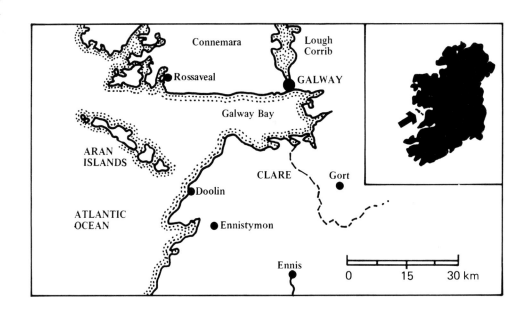

ridge rises to the west of this bay widening the island once more before it slopes gently to the Atlantic at its north-western tip. Inishmaan (*Inis Meáin* – the middle island), lies to the south east of Inishmore across two kilometres of open sea known as Gregory's Sound. It is much smaller than Inishmore, and is more compact in its shape, extending five kilometres from east to west. Inisheer (*Inis Oírr* – the eastern island) is even smaller being an almost regular square with a total area of ten square kilometres. The broad sweep of the South Sound isolates Inisheer from the mainland of Co. Clare, ten kilometres away. A number of small islands complete the Aran group. Rock Island, at the north western tip of Inishmore, is, as the name suggests, a bare rocky surface, inhabited only by the staff who tend the lighthouse erected there in the middle of the nineteenth century. The nearby Brannock Island (*Oileán dá Bhranóg* – the island of the two small ravens) is uninhabited, its limited pastures being grazed by a herd of donkeys. The sandy soils of Straw Island, at the mouth of Killeany Bay, were once utilised to grow rye. It too is uninhabited though an automated lighthouse stands at its western point, a beacon to guide shipping to the piers at Kilronan and Killeany.

Isolation is part of life on Aran. In good weather conditions there is a considerable traffic with the mainland but gale-force winds frequently sever the shipping links and prevent contact with the outside world for weeks on end. The shelving sea bed around the islands makes for a particularly treacherous sea during a storm. The waves break more than a kilometre from the shore, sending gigantic white combers rushing towards the rocks. Life is at its grimmest on the islands when they are stormbound. Communications are cut off, mail and visitors fail to arrive and supplies of food frequently run low. The community is obliged to rely on its own resources to provide for essential needs. Illness during storm conditions is a terrifying prospect. Often a crossing must be attempted, regardless of wind or wave, when a patient is in need of hospitalisation. The islanders grimly joke that a patient in his terror forgets about his illness until he reaches the safety of Rossaveal on the mainland – where his condition immediately deteriorates once more.

For the summer visitor the journey to Aran is a much more pleasant affair. A three hour cruise from Galway city across calm seas brings him within sight of the islands. As the boat approaches its destination, the twin humps of Inishmore, often blurred by mist or haze, assume a more distinct outline. The grey uniformity of the surface rock is the dominant visual tone and only gradually does the observer pick out the golden sandy beaches flecked with the white froth of the breaking waves.

A little higher on the slopes the white and grey washed houses take shape, straggling in an irregular line along the lee side of the ridge. The boat rounds the point of Straw Island and the harbour is now visible, fishing craft in their berths or at anchor, the black crescents of upturned curraghs near the beach, and the confusion of men, animals and goods on the pier head. In the nineteenth century the journey had to be made by curragh, a colourful and exciting experience for the stranger.

RACING WITH THE WAVES

J. M. Synge visited the Aran Islands each summer during the years 1898 to 1902, and he lived with families on Inishmore and Inishmaan. His book, *The Aran Islands,* is an account of life on the islands at that time. In this excerpt, Synge describes a curragh ride in rough seas on his way to the islands.

WE SET OFF. IT WAS A four-oared curragh, and I was given the last seat so as to leave the stern for the man who was steering with an oar, worked at right angles to the others by an extra thole-pin in the stern gunnel.

When we had gone about a hundred yards they ran up a bit of a sail in the bow and the pace became extraordinarily rapid.

The shower had passed over and the wind had fallen, but large, magnificently brilliant waves were rolling down on us at right angles to our course.

Every instant the steersman whirled us round with a sudden stroke of his oar, the prow reared up and then fell into the next furrow with a crash, throwing up masses of spray. As it did so, the stern in its turn was thrown up, and both the steersman, who let go his oar and clung with both hands to the gunnel, and myself, were lifted high up above the sea.

The wave passed, we regained our course and rowed violently for a few yards, when the same manoeuvre had to be repeated. As we worked out into the sound we began to meet another class of waves, that could be seen for some distance towering above the rest.

When one of these came in sight, the first effort was to get beyond its reach. The steersman began crying out in Gaelic

'Siubhal, siubhal' ('Run, run'), and sometimes, when the mass was gliding towards us with horrible speed, his voice rose to a shriek. Then the rowers themselves took up the cry, and the curragh seemed to leap and quiver with the frantic terror of a beast till the wave passed behind it or fell with a crash beside the stern.

It was in this racing with the waves that our chief danger lay. If the wave could be avoided, it was better to do so, but if it overtook us while we were trying to escape, and caught us on the broadside, our destruction was certain. I could see the steersman quivering with the excitement of his task, for any error in his judgment would have swamped us.

We had one narrow escape. A wave appeared high above the rest, and there was the usual moment of intense exertion. It was of no use, and in an instant the wave seemed to be hurling itself upon us. With a yell of rage the steersman struggled with his oar to bring our prow to meet it. He had almost succeeded, when there was a crash and rush of water round us. I felt as if I had been struck upon the back with knotted ropes. White foam gurgled round my knees and eyes. The curragh reared up, swaying and trembling for a moment, and then fell safely into the furrow.

This was our worst moment, though more than once, when several waves came so closely together that we had no time to regain control of the canoe between them, we had some dangerous work. Our lives depended upon the skill and courage of the men, as the life of the rider or swimmer is often in his own hands, and the excitement of the struggle was too great to allow time for fear.

I enjoyed the passage. Down in this shallow trough of canvas that bent and trembled with the motion of the men, I had a far more intimate feeling of the glory and power of the waves than I have ever known in a steamer.

the physical landscape

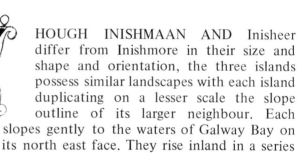

HOUGH INISHMAAN AND Inisheer differ from Inishmore in their size and shape and orientation, the three islands possess similar landscapes with each island duplicating on a lesser scale the slope outline of its larger neighbour. Each slopes gently to the waters of Galway Bay on its north east face. They rise inland in a series of terraces before dipping once more to meet the Atlantic waves on their south west sides.

Inishmore shows the characteristic Aran landscape in its most extreme form. A series of eight distinct terraces, each with a well developed scarp or cliff, rises inland like a giant's staircase on each of the two hill masses which make up the greater part of the island's surface. These 'steps' rise to an altitude of 124 metres at Oghil, the highest point in the whole of the Aran group, and they attain an altitude of 108 metres in a parallel sequence on the western hill at Onaght. From these central heights the land dips gently westward to the coast before plunging abruptly over sheer cliffs to the Atlantic waves below. The visually impressive scarps which front the steps, are minor limestone cliffs ranging from three to five metres in height. The scarps are most sheer and the terraces narrowest near the north-east shore. Inland, the terraces are much wider, the most extensive pair being each one kilometre wide in parts. These latter terraces are well sheltered and are the sites for all but one of the islands fourteen 'villages'. In the low neck of the island at Port Murvey a single terrace offers a site to Gort na gCapall, the only village on the western or Atlantic side of the island.

Inishmaan and Inisheer display a similar sequence of steps but their cliffs are much lower and less continuous than those in Inishmore.

Within each of the islands, there are three distinct types of landscape. Each has extensive areas of low lying sand dunes on the north shore, the sand giving way to shingle and gravel on Inishmore. Inland the slope rises in a series of terraces which have been favoured sites for settlement and agriculture. Finally, south west of the summits, there are areas of sparsely vegetated rock known in each case as "the back of the island" and utilised, only in a limited way, as winter grazing.

The most visually impressive landscape feature in the Aran group, the feature which binds all three islands into a geographical and geological unity, is the expanse of bare limestone pavement found on each.

The limestones of Ireland were formed 350 million years ago when much of the country was submerged under a warm, shallow sea. This sea teemed with marine life forms whose calcium rich bones and shells fell to the sea bed when they died. The pressure of the sea water combined with natural cementing agents to bond these layers of shells and bones into the rock we know as limestone.

Limestone is classified as a sedimentary rock by geologists, which means that it is formed from particles of material, or sediments, which settled, or came to rest, at the bottom of the sea. The Aran limestones contain many fossils, the preserved remains of some of the marine organisms which went to make up the rock. Within the limestone we can easily identify layers or strata and the bedding planes which separate them. The Aran beds are tilted gently to the south west. In fact this 'dip' slope of the rock corresponds with the gentle slope from the summit to the cliffs at the "back of the island".

In the Aran islands, and in the similar Burren area of North Clare the massive blocks of limestone are exposed at the surface and are almost completely devoid of any soil cover. This type of bare limestone landscape is known as Karst, taking its name from the Karst area of Yugoslavia where geologists first studied it.

It seemed possible that the Aran islands did not always have a barren limestone surface. The ice sheets which melted at the end of the Ice Age 10,000 years ago probably left a blanket of boulder clay (a mixture of crushed rock, sand and gravel) over most of the islands. Bad farming practices combined with the power of the wind and the rain have resulted in the erosion of this covering and in the exposure of the limestone beneath.

The chemicals contained in limestone are easily dissolved by rain water which sometimes contains a weak carbonic acid. The rainwater attacks exposed limestone along joints and cracks and lines of weakness enlarging them into wide, deep fissures. Annual rainfall totals are high in the islands but the water quickly percolates down through the fissures and the landscape presents an arid face, weathered to a remarkable crazy pavement effect.

The massive grey limestones of Aran are interbedded with thin bands of shale, a rock which has a much greater resistance to the erosive action of rainwater. This difference in the rates of erosion of the two rocks creates the stepped landscape which is character-istic of Inishmore in particular.

The absence of surface water is the most striking feature of the drainage pattern on the islands. Rainfall disappears through the fissures almost as soon as it has fallen and surface streams frequently dry up altogether in summer. An example of such an intermittent stream is found at Sruthán on Inishmore.

Although water can pass freely through limestone it is unable to penetrate the shale beds beneath and its downward movement is halted. It then collects at the bedding plane which separates the limestone from the shale and flows along the dip slope of the rock as an underground stream. Such streams eventually emerge on the slopes at the base of the limestone scarps where they provide a water supply for the villages.

Droughts frequently occur during the summer months when rain may not fall for several weeks at a time. Surface streams dry up completely and the islanders have difficulty in finding sufficient water to supply the animals in their fields. Since the 1920's the Inishmore farmers, aided by Government grants, have constructed numerous rain troughs in their fields. These troughs are fashioned from slabs of limestone pointed with cement and each has a surface area of about six square metres. In order to increase the catchment potential of these troughs an apron, or platform, is built onto one or more sides of the trough. This apron, six to nine square metres in area, slopes at an angle of about thirty degrees to the lip of the trough allowing any water which lands on its surface to drain into the trough. The surface of the apron is cemented over in order to prevent the precious rain water from seeping down through the limestone blocks of which it is built. On the smaller islands there is less need for these rain troughs as each individual's house is located much nearer to his fields and there is less labour involved in carrying water to the grazing animals.

An interesting feature of drainage on Aran are the turloughs which are found at An Turloch Mór and Poll na gCapall on Inishmore. A turlough (*tur loch* — a dry lake) is an impermanent lake which occurs in a shallow depression in the limestone. When heavy rainfall occurs the level of permanent water saturation in the ground, known as the water table, rises rapidly and the turlough fills up, often in a matter of hours. During a period of exceptionally heavy rainfall the turlough may flood surrounding fields. In a dry summer, however, the water table will drop allowing the water of the lake to drain through fissures in the lake bed. The turlough will shrink to pond size, or it may, in a prolonged drought, dry up completely, providing good temporary grazing for cattle and sheep.

THE WORK OF THE SEA

The south-west face of each of the Aran islands lies open to the great Atlantic breakers which are driven shorewards by the prevailing south-west winds. Mountainous waves batter the islands in Autumn and Winter, waves which have travelled across the wide Atlantic and which are meeting with resistance for the first time. The erosive power of these waves is great even in calm weather. In storm conditions they exert a tremendous pressure on the cliffs, hurling boulders and rock fragments against them, and occasionally tossing huge rocks right over the cliff top.

Inishmore is edged on its west side with a continuous line of remarkably sheer cliffs. The coastlines of Inishmaan and Inisheer are lower, but where cliffs occur on these islands they also tend to be sheer. The clean vertical face of the cliffs, free of any rock outcrops, allows the islanders to fish from the top with a heavily weighted line. This practice of cliff-top fishing for wrasse, known locally as rockfish, was common in the past. In the mid-nineteenth century a tragedy occurred at Glassan Rock, near the south eastern end of Inishmore, which is still recalled in the island today. Fifteen men from Killeany village who were fishing from a ledge were swept into the sea by a freak wave and were drowned.

Above — The shifting sand dunes of Inisheer are believed to have buried a number of ancient settlements. Teampall Chaomhain has escaped the same fate only because the sand is shovelled out of the building each year on June 14th, the saint's feast day.

Left — Limestone pavement eroding under the influence of the sea spray. Rock pools formed in this way are common on Inishmore.

THEARAN ISLANDS   19

Almost every household in the little village was bereaved of a husband or son in the disaster, which, according to popular lore, was occasioned by the fact that the men had not attended mass on the day in question which was a church Holy Day.

Other features of note on the highland coast of Inishmore are the sea arch at Poll na Brioscarnach and the strange natural 'swimming pool' at Poll na bPéist. This latter feature is a rectangular basin in the rock, into which the sea flows through a submarine passage, the legendary haunt of a sea monster. When, in a storm, water swells through the access passage, it shoots a jet into the air not unlike the spouting of a monster. Poll na bPéist is just one of a number of such puffing holes found on Inishmore and Inishmaan.

All three islands have storm beaches on their southern and south western shores. The storm beaches are lines of massive boulders which have been tossed over the cliff top in severe storms, coming to rest in a jumbled line — a visible testament to the power of the angry sea.

The more sheltered north-east shores of the islands present a contrasting face. The three islands slope, or step, gently down to Galway Bay and the sea bed shelves gradually towards the Connemara mainland. Even up to three kilometres north of Inishmore depths of less than ten fathoms can be recorded. This lowland coast has been shaped by marine deposition rather than by erosion. Extensive beaches of shingle and sand have been laid down here and the north east corner of each island is a landscape of shifting sand dunes. The roof of the ancient church, Teaghlach Éinne, near Iarairne is on the same level as the top of the dunes which surround it and the church of St. Cavan of Inisheer has to be regularly cleared of sand drifts. The dunes are devoid of houses, roads and fences and are held as commonage by groups of island families. An Trá Mór, the magnificent stretch of beach at the eastern end of Inishmore, is a lagoon in the making as it is gradually being cut off from the open sea by sandpits. Loch Port Charruch and Loch Dearg, on the same island, are lagoons which were cut off from the sea by shingle bars.

CLIMATE

The hallmark of the daily weather on the islands, as elsewhere in Ireland, is its changeability. The sky may cloud up or clear to a radiant blue within a matter of hours and a rainy day is often interrupted by a few hours of sunshine when the glistening rock pavements create the illusion of a landscape of shallow lakes. As one local man observed, "the four seasons all come in one day".

The climate of Aran, like that of Ireland generally is oceanic and it is characteristically mild, moist and equable. The influence of the ocean is important, as summer temperatures seldom exceed 16°C due to the cool breezes. Similarly, winter temperatures seldom drop below 5°C and frost and snow are a rarity. Low annual and daily temperature ranges are typical of the islands' climate. The North Atlantic Drift, a warm ocean current which originates in the Gulf of Mexico, flows along the west coast of Ireland and is particularly effective in keeping winter temperatures well above freezing point.

The pattern of rainfall on Aran is broadly similar to that found throughout the western part of Ireland. Ireland lies in the direct path of the south-west winds, winds which are laden with moisture because they have passed over a relatively warm ocean where constant evaporation goes on. West coast locations received the brunt of this rainfall and the Aran islands have a high annual total of rainfall relative to places in the centre of the country or on the east coast. The mountainous Galway mainland, being higher, has an even greater annual rainfall than the Aran group, the highest point of which stands only 124 metres above sea level.

This table gives the monthly average rainfall (mm.) and temperatures (degrees Celsius) for the Aran Islands.

Jan.	Feb.	Mar.	Apr.	May	June	July	Aug.	Sept.	Oct.	Nov.	Dec.
116	79	73	62	65	73	83	105	119	126	115	136
5.8	6.0	7.7	9.0	11.3	14.0	15.2	15.3	13.8	11.0	8.4	6.8

Rainfall is well distributed throughout the year — even the driest month, April, has a substantial amount — but the nature of the surface rock exaggerates the effects of even a short drought and dry sunny summers result in rapid evaporation from the shallow soils.

Most typical of late autumn, winter and spring is a misty foggy type of weather when a fine drizzle falls for hours on end. Such a day, mild but very wetting, is described as a "lá bog" or a soft day. Fogs frequently hang about the shores of Galway Bay proving hazardous to sailor and fisherman alike. Stories are told of currach crews being enveloped in dense fog and losing their way, rowing until they dropped from exhaustion.

The first lighthouse to be erected on Aran was built in the early

19th century at the highest point of Inishmore near Dún Eochla. This lighthouse is a prominent feature of the Inishmore skyline from almost any vantage point on the island. It was, however, too high to be of any use as a beacon in foggy conditions and even in clear conditions ships lying in close to the cliffs on the south side could not see the light which might have warned them of their danger. This lighthouse was soon replaced by the structure on Rock Island. A similar lighthouse was erected at Pointe an Fhardarus, the south east tip of Inisheer, to mark the other extremity of the islands.

On a clear day the view from the cliffs of Inishmore or Inishmaan is unsurpassable. The absence of pollution and the constant sea breezes give a remarkable clarity to the air and it is easy to pick out the long sloping shoreline of Co. Clare, and, far to the south, the promontory of Kerry Head on the other side of the Shannon. It may also be possible to see, in the right meteorological conditions, the celebrated mirage known variously as Hy Brasil or Tír na nÓg. This illusion has been frequently observed, lying between the Irish Coast and the horizon, and folklore has represented it as being, among other things, the Garden of Eden, the land of eternal youth and a lost Atlantis-like continent.

The Aran islands are low-lying and they seem to crouch before the winds which whip across them in winter. Gales are a frequent occurrence and the south westerlies are often accompanied by mountainous seas. Winds registering Force 10 and Force 11 on the Beaufort scale often buffet the islands in autumn and winter. Some of the worst gales on record have come in late September and early October. The absence of settlement on the south and west side of the ridges on all three islands becomes understandable when one has experienced a storm in Aran. As long ago as 1684 Roderick O'Flaherty recorded in his *Chorographical Description of West Connacht* that a gigantic wave swept across the low neck of Inishmore between Gort na gCapall and Kilmurvey in 1640 A.D. Independent evidence records the occurrence of an earthquake on the north-west coasts of Europe at about that time. It seems possible that the wave which O'Flaherty noted in his history was a tidal wave associated with these earth tremors.

SOILS

It is thought that the islands may once have had an adequate soil cover though today they present a largely barren rock surface.

Such soils, if they did exist were probably formed on a parent material of boulder clay which the retreating ice sheets left behind 100,000 years ago.

The soils now found on the islands are the result of the weathering of exposed shale beds. Natural soils have been unable to develop on the limestone pavement because water dissolves rather than breaks up the rock. The layer of rock fragments and powder which has developed on the shale and which bacteria and other organisms change into soil, has never formed on the limestone.

ERRATICS

Great round boulders of granite are found scattered about the pavement at the eastern and western ends of Inishmore. The crystalline nature of these rocks contrasts strongly with the uniform grey of the limestone on which they rest. Folktales explain them as the missiles of an angry giant who lived in Connemara, an explanation not too far removed from the scientific facts. They are, in fact, glacial erratics, huge boulders which were moved from their place of origin by the advancing ice sheets and dumped unceremoniously when the temperatures rose once again and a thaw set in. These erratics have been incorporated into the stone walls of the island and some were shaped into Bullauns − rocks hollowed into a basin which may have been used as a bowl in which to grind corn by the early Christian monks or by pre-Christian farmers.

VEGETATION

We will never know what kind of natural vegetation might have evolved on the Aran islands had man never set foot on them. Man has destroyed soil and made soil; he has fertilised the land and exhausted the land; he has tilled fields and built walls and broken the flat surface of the pavements. His activities have had an influence on the various habitats available to plants. Other factors such as the nature of the rock, the distribution, depth and type of the soil, the relief and slope of the land, the amount and distribution of rainfall and the daily and yearly temperature patterns have all influenced the evolution of the local vegetation.

Four distinct habitats can be identified. On the limestone pavements, soil can be found only in the fissures or grykes which crisscross the landscape. This habitat offers limited soil and light and there is an absence of permanent water at root level though rainwater regularly passes through the fissures. A variety of ferns thrive on this habitat, particularly the Maiden Hair Fern and the Hart's Tongue Fern. Flowering plants which can tolerate the alkaline salts in the pockets of soil are common, and rare species such as Alpine Spring Gentian can also be found. The fissures also support a number of varieties of dwarfed trees, including hazel, hawthorn and blackthorn which enjoy a stunted growth up to ground level.

In many places the pavement environment has been modified by man's creation of soil. This distinctive habitat displays the ordinary range of meadow grasses and flowers as well as some rarer lime-tolerant plants. On many of the scarp faces a growth of ivy is found and it also thrives on the ruined walls of dwelling houses. At the base of some scarps, where springs issue from the rock, hydrophytes are common.

Thirdly, the sand-dunes provide a severely limited environment for some varieties of sedges and grasses. The shifting sands are suitable only to plants with a brief life-cycle whose processes of growth and reproduction can be accomplished in the shortest space of time. Water drains quickly through the porous sands and the wind regularly whips up sand storms. For these reasons the dune plants must develop deep root systems, or a network of

The surface of the limestone pavement offers neither soil nor shelter nor moisture for plant growth. Only in the fissures and crevasses has soil accumulated and is there shelter to be found from the wind.

The remains of a dolmen on Inishmaan. This tomb is one of the indications that the islands were inhabited in the Megalithic period.

roots which extend laterally, serving to anchor the plant as well as to seek out moisture. Man-made walls provide some shelter and allow plants to establish themselves.

The shore between High Water Mark and Low Water Mark is a fourth habitat. Algaes of the usual varieties are found some of which, such as kelp and bladder-wrack, are of economic importance. These seaweeds grow better on the north and east shores than they do on the more exposed western shores.

The absence of large trees on all three islands is visually one of the most striking features. Folklore and local placenames would seem to indicate that the islands were once wooded. The place name Eochla, for instance, is thought to refer to a stand of yew trees. It is unlikely though that anything other than shrubs or scrubby woodland ever grew on the islands due to a general lack of shelter from the prevailing south westerly winds. The few trees and bushes one meets with on the bend of the main road west of Cowrugh on Inishmore, are stunted in their growth and, in their branch formation, lean heavily away from the wind. Inishmaan has a single tree, Inisheer has none at all. The only stand of trees in the whole island group are those which were planted in the grounds of the rectory at Kilronan in the late 19th century.

the ɔúɔs of αʀαɔ

HE ARAN ISLANDS bear the print of continuous occupation since the very first settlers came to Ireland several thousand years before the birth of Christ. The earliest of the Aran remains are thought to date from the Megalithic period when the inhabitants of Ireland erected great tombs of standing stones, known as dolmens. From this period the islands now contain only a wedge grave at Baile Sean on Inishmore, a ruined dolmen on Inishmaan, some lesser remains on Inisheer and a Megalithic settlement buried beneath the shifting sands of Iararirne. This settlement lay exposed and was studied around the middle of the 19th century. The great stone forts are undoubtedly the most impressive of the remains found on the islands today. As one approaches Inishmore the primitive outline of Dún Eochla appears on the skyline. Further west is the barbaric magnificence of the Dún Aengus site and Dún Conor dominates from its hilltop position, the whole landscape of Inishmaan. They are massive structures of dry-stone masonry, a building technique widely employed in the Celtic period, perhaps even in the pre-Celtic period. The technology of these early builders did not include the use of mortar, that is any filling or binding agent such as mud or cement. Mortared buildings came into Ireland only with the advent of the Normans in the late 12th century. Mortared structures such as the castle begin to assume a place in the landscape from that date onwards. The dry-stone of the fort building however, is still used by the ordinary Aran farmer in breaking down and building up some of the 11,000 kilometres

of stone walls which divide up his island into a patchwork of tiny
fields.

The fort builders used the material which was all around them,
that is, limestone, a rock that is very easily split and shaped. Like
all Aran men they knew how to make best use of the local rock
and their structures were carefully built to withstand weathering
and time. Stones are massive at the base of the walls and they
rise layer upon layer, bracing one another, through careful
selection and skilful placing. The wall of each fort was constructed by first of all building up two walls with a space between them
and filling in this space with limestone rubble and smaller rocks.
Each wall is terraced so that while it is six metres wide at the base
it narrows to about two metres wide at the top. Within some of
the forts are the jumbled ruins of dwelling houses, stone buildings
of dry stone construction. Some also contain souterrains, underground passages leading to a point outside the walls. These may
have been used for the storage of food or as an exit route in an
emergency.

Though the origins of the forts are clouded in mystery, scholars
now agree that they may not be as ancient as was first thought.
They may have existed as early as the 8th century B.C. but it
seems more likely that they were built in the 1st or 2nd century
B.C. and that they were used throughout the early Christian
period and even into the Middle Ages. Similar stone forts were
being constructed elsewhere in the country as late as the year
1100 A.D. and evidence from Co. Clare suggests that they were
in daily use even in the 16th century.

Island folklore claims that the forts were built by the Fir
Bolg, a prehistoric tribe who invaded the country but were
defeated by subsequent invaders. The Fir Bolg then fled from the
mainland and sought refuge on Aran and other west-coast islands.
The legends say that they built the forts as a defensive measure
as they prepared to make their last stand. Those who put forward
this claim point to the massiveness of the stone walls, to the sites
being on or near hilltops and to the barrenness of the Aran landscape as proof. Why should they have come here unless they had
been forced to, such scholars say. They forget, however, that the
Ireland of even one thousand years ago was a country of woodland, bog and swamp where communication was difficult and
dangerous. Coastal locations were regarded as prime sites. The land
of Aran was probably not always as barren as it is today and the
islands were not merely a wasteland with no possible use other

◄The massive wall of Dún Dú-chathair seen from inside the fortification. The rough dry stone wall rises by means of two ramparts to a total height of 6 metres. In the foreground can be seen the ruins of the clochans or stone huts which were the probable dwellings of the original inhabitants of the duns.

Below — The chevaux-de-frise of Dun Aengus. This remarkable barrier of razor-sharp standing stones was certainly a defensive measure. A small band of defenders could, from the safety of the third wall, in the background, inflict heavy losses on enemies who were attempting to pick their way through this solid 'barbed wire'.

than for defensive purposes. The tradition which associates Dun Aengus with the Firbolg Prince Aengus may be no more than a few centuries old. But most important of all is the fact that none of the Dun sites contain a source of fresh water and so these structures can hardly have been intended as refuges which could hold out against a long siege. The building of the Duns must have required a huge expenditure of time, manpower and materials, and can hardly have been the work of a defeated people making a last ditch stand on an Atlantic cliff-top. It is much more likely that they are the proud monuments of a prosperous and aggressive people. Their owners were probably rich farmers, as all of the forts are situated close to some of the best agricultural land on their respective islands. Early writers, such as Roderick O'Flaherty in the 17th century, described the forts in terms of the number of cattle which they might have held, a probable clue to their original use.

Thirty to forty thousand forts were scattered throughout Ireland in the pre-Norman period. They were the dwellings of the 'strong' farmers in each district. In fertile parts of the country the fort, known as a Lios or a Rath, was made up of one or more earthen banks. In the western part of the country the fort was known as a dun or cathair or caiseal and was built of stone. Stone was readily available and it is an easily used material and the building of the walls helped in the clearing of the land. There were probably other cathairs and duns on the Aran Islands which were not as sturdily built or not as well preserved as those that survived. The remains of stone walls at Baile na Sean and Baile na mBocht on Inishmore may have once been part of the walls of a number of Duns. These, and other forts, crumbled or were dismantled to provide building stone for houses or walls. The Aran duns are all large and strongly built and it has been suggested that they were the homes of clan groups rather than of individual families. Then, as now, an individual or group with a surplus of wealth tended to convert it into a prestigious monument usually in a prominent site.

There was, however, some consideration of defence present in the minds of the dun builders. The sites, on hill tops and cliff tops, the strength of the walls and the presence around some forts of *chevaux de frise*, or lines of strategically placed standing stones, would seem to indicate a definite defensive intent. The lack of fresh water meant that they were unsuitable for a prolonged siege so they were probably used as a refuge during the short-lived attacks by pirates or mainland raiders.

The Aran forts are of two kinds, Dún Conor and Dún Eochla are examples of hill forts, and Dún Eonaghta, while not at the highest point of its hill, is located very near the summit. Dún Dúchathair is a perfect example of a promontory fort, that is, a fort built on a headland which needs only a single wall as it has the cliffs for protection on three sides. Dún Aengus has elements of both the hill-top and promontory types. In all, there are remains of seven forts on the islands, four on Inishmore, two on Inishmaan and one on Inisheer. It should be remembered however, that almost all of the forts were repaired by the Board of Works in the 1890's, using the best knowledge and craftsmanship available at that time. The buttresses which bolster up the inner wall of Dún Aengus were built at that time and the regular outline of the walls of all of the forts is probably a false picture of what they originally looked like.

DÚN AENGUS

Dún Aengus is the most impressive, and the most famous, of all the Aran forts. It is a spectacular structure, both in the enormous scale of its walls and in the precarious cliff top site it occupies. It consists of four roughly concentric walls, all of which back onto a cliff edge with a sheer drop of several hundred feet to the pounding Atlantic waves below. One may be tempted, on first viewing Dún Aengus, to regard it as the remaining half of an ordinary ringfort, the rest of which has been destroyed by the erosion of the cliff on which it is set. But it is highly unlikely that there ever was "another half". The plan of the fort could hardly be bettered, making use, as it does, of the cliff edge as an absolute protection against attack from the west side.

The innermost of the four enclosures resembles half of an oval with an east-west diameter of forty-two metres. It is surrounded by a wall, four metres wide at the base, which rises up to six metres in two terraces. On the east side a doorway, whose massive lintels still remain in place, afforded entry and exit to the dun-dwellers. In the centre of the enclosure, backing onto the lip of the cliff, is a rectangular platform, twelve metres by nine, which is nothing more than a natural rock outcrop though it has been described as a man-made 'table' or 'altar'.

Outside this enclosure is a second wall which follows the curve of the inner wall before extending eastward to take in a consider-

Dún Aengus from the air, showing the sequence of four walls. The cliff top position, magnificent and precarious, seems to imply a defensive intent by the dún builders. The main enclosure is horse-shoe shaped and was never at any time a circular ring fort as some scholars have claimed. In the centre of the horse-shoe, at the very cliff edge is a remarkable 'table' of rock, a natural outcrop. The sheer nature of the Aran cliffs and the well defined bedding planes of the rock can be clearly seen.

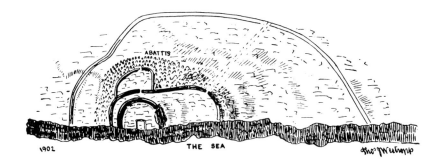

ABATTIS

1902   THE SEA   Thos JWestropp

able area of land before finally meeting the cliff face. Further out are fragments of a third wall which once followed the general outline of the other walls. It is believed that this third wall was demolished in order to provide stone for the building of the fourth wall — a massive structure which extends 400 metres and encloses a D-shaped plot, 4.5 hectares in area.

Between the third and fourth walls are the well preserved remains of a *chevaux de frise*. This is an arrangement of closely spaced standing stones, some up to 1.5 metres in height, which slope toward one another, making a passage through them slow and difficult. John O'Donovan of the Ordnance Survey wrote this description of the *chevaux de frise* at Dún Aengus in 1839: "Some of these stones appear at a distance like soldiers making the onset, and many of them are so sharp that if one fell against them they would run him through. This army of stones would appear to have been intended by the Bolgae of Aran to answer the same purpose as the modern chevaux de Frise, now generally used in making a retrenchment to stop cavalry; but these stones were never intended to keep off horses, as no horses could come near the place without 'breaking their legs'. They must have been, therefore, used for keeping off men, and very well adapted they are for this purpose, for a few men standing on the outer wall just described, could by casting stones, kill hundreds of invaders while attempting to pass through this army of sharp stones."

Even today, after centuries of exposure to the weather, some of these standing stones remain razor sharp to the touch. The *chevaux de frise* probably extended right round the original third wall of the fort but it is preserved only on the north side. One can only wonder as to why the dun dwellers decided to build a fourth wall outside the *chevaux de frise* and to do so tore down the easily defended third wall. The size of the enclosure and the sheer length of the fourth wall would have made it almost impossible to defend so we can only conclude that this last wall was built much later than the others, during a peaceful era when the old fortifications were no longer regarded as essential. If this is so the eleven acres enclosure may have been envisaged as an elaborate cattle pen rather than an additional defensive measure.

The name Dún Aengus has been traditionally associated with the mythical Firbolg prince Aengus and some stories have it that the fort is the resting place of the Firbolg warriors who lie there awaiting the call to arms once more.

OTHER FORTS

Dún Dúchathair (The Black Fort) is situated on a promontory to the east of Dún Aengus. Here the cliffs are much lower, but they surround the fort on three sides affording it excellent protection. The fort itself consists of a single roughly constructed wall, sixty metres in length, which runs across the neck of the promontory providing an effective and easily defended barrier. The wall, like that of Dún Aengus, rises in two steps and a *chevaux de frise* of standing stones on the landward side combine with the sheer cliffs to make this a secure defensive site.

Dún Eochla (the fort of the Yew Wood) is a well preserved example of a hill fort. It is situated near to the highest point of Inishmore commanding a magnificent view of the sea approaches on all sides of the island. Dún Eochla consists of two roughly concentric massively built walls, the inner having a diameter of 23 metres. Within this inner circle is a large mount of loose stone which was built up during reconstruction work in the late nineteenth century. These stones are believed to be the last remnants of the clochans or stone huts which formerly housed the occupants of the dun.

Dún Eonaghta (the fort of the Eonaght tribe) is situated on the western hill of Inishmore near to a summit or altitude of 108 metres. It also is a circular hill fort but consists of one wall only. The name Eonaght is believed to be associated with a Munster tribe who are reputed to have occupied part of the island at one time. Dún Eonaghta is situated within reach of some relatively good agricultural land and overlooks the site which was later chosen for one of the major monasteries of Aran. The fort itself was probably the residence of a farming clan group.

Dún Conor, on Inishmaan, is the largest of all the Aran ring forts, and is the finest example of a hill fort in Ireland. It occupies a splendid site on the north side of the central summit of the island. The enclosed area five thousand five hundred square metres in extent, is surrounded by a wall up to six metres high in parts. As in the other forts, this wall has a wide base, and it rises in two steps so that it is much narrower at the top. An outer wall takes the form of a semi-circle around the north and east sides of the fort. This wall does not extend to the south or west sides of the inner circle as a steep rocky slope on these sides probably convinced the dun builders that the natural defences were already adequate. At the northernmost corner of this outer wall there is a small walled enclosure which may have acted as a defensive gateway. Within the fort are the remains of structures which must have originally been clochans or dry-stone beehive huts.

The land around Dún Conor is among the best available on Inishmaan and many of the island farmers own fields in the vicinity of the fort. From the topmost rampart one can see how the fields with their stone walls follow the lines of the fortification.

In a crevice in the wall of the fort, a mainland man named Malley who had accidentally killed his father in a fit of passion, was hidden by the islanders for several months before he managed to make good his escape to America. This incident, reputed to have occurred sometime during the nineteenth century, was related to J. M. Synge. The playwright was much taken with the story and he later used it as the inspiration for the plot of his famous comedy *The Playboy of the Western World*.

The other ringfort of Inishmaan, Dún Moher, also known as Dún Fhearbhaigh is less impressive than Dún Conor, being a smaller D-shaped structure. It too is situated in good farmland and was also the probable dwelling of a tribal farming group.

The hilltop fort of Dún Formna is situated near to the highest point of Inisheer, a commanding position over the occupied northern part of the island. Only one wall of this fort has survived and though considerable in its extent it is less massive in its construction than that of any of the other forts. Within Dún Formna a castle was constructed in the sixteenth century by the O'Brien clan of Co. Clare, who ruled the Aran Islands at that time. This castle probably utilised the old line of the Dun as an outer defensive barrier. These two buildings, their origins separated by at least one thousand years of history, share the prime site of the island, and the building techniques used in each contrast strongly. The mortared masonry of the castle is a product of the Norman invasion. The dry-stone masonry of the dun wall that surrounds it is more primitive perhaps, but it makes for an equally sturdy fortification.

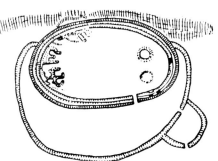

Plan of Dun Conor, Inishmaan. The enclosed area is 5,500 sq. metres in extent.

INISHEER

We first drop anchor, beyond the pier,
Off the first island called Inisheer,
Where all the islandmen and women
Wear bright-knit shawls and well-patched homespun,
The women with rainbows round their shoulders,
The oarsmen strong and grey as boulders.
The currachs that lie along the strand
Are hoisted up. Black new moons walk the sand
And down where the waves break in white lace.
The bobbing boats all plunge and race
And row right under the steamer's bows —
Then back they ride with homely cargoes.

Seamus Heaney

ara na naomh

HRISTIANITY FIRST CAME to Ireland in the early part of the fifth century A.D. and it is believed to have been brought to Aran by St. Enda who founded a monastery at Killeany, on Inishmore, in the year 490 A.D. Enda's foundation was one of the earliest and one of the most important monasteries of the period. It became famous throughout Ireland and holy men flocked there to lead a life of study and prayer. Many of those trained in the monastic life of Aran later founded monasteries of their own elsewhere in Ireland or on the continent of Europe. Several of the Fathers of the early Irish Church studied in Aran or visited the islands which were widely known as Ara na Naomh — Aran of the Saints.

A typical monastery would have centred on a group of small churches where the monks could pray privately or in small groups. The monks would have lived in huts or cells nearby, which, in Aran would have taken the form of beehive huts called clochans, built of dry-stone masonry. The monastery would also contain workshops for blacksmiths and scribes and, perhaps, a building to house visitors and travellers. The whole monastic settlement would have been surrounded by an earthen bank or stone wall. The monastic site would usually have been marked by stone crosses. At first these crosses were cut into the face of any convenient boulder but later the stone was shaped into the form of a cross. As the skill of the stone-cutters developed over the centuries they began to decorate the crosses with elaborate designs and lettering. Many magnificent examples of these High Crosses can still be seen throughout Ireland.

The monks lived under a strict rule devoting their lives to work and prayer. At set times during the day and night they gathered in the churches to pray. On Wednesdays and Fridays they fasted taking only one meal each day at evening time. Lent was observed as a time of special fasting and penance.

The monastery farm provided for all the needs of the community. The monks grew corn which they milled by hand to make bread. They kept herds of cattle and sheep, and in some cases, chickens and bees. Where possible fish from the lakes and sea was part of their diet.

Many of the monasteries had schools attached which attracted students from Britain and Europe. Some of the monks worked as scribes copying the gospels by hand onto sheets of cured cowhide called vellum. Annals, accounts of the important events which occurred in the locality each year, were also compiled. Manuscripts of this kind were almost certainly compiled on Aran but none has survived. However many beautifully coloured and intricately lettered books from monasteries elsewhere in Ireland are preserved in museums and libraries.

Monastic life flourished in Ireland, and in Aran, during the centuries following Enda's death, a period often referred to as The Golden Age. Aran contains the remains of two major monastic settlements, one situated at Killeany on Inishmore, the other at Onaght, further west on the same island. Numerous other remains are found in between these sites and on Inishmaan and Inisheer.

KILLEANY

Enda, the patron saint of Aran, is believed to have been born in Leinster and to have been converted to a Christian vocation through the efforts of his sister who was a nun. After founding a small monastery in the Boyne Valley he lived in Scotland for a number of years before returning to establish foundations in other parts of Ireland. Finally he came to Aran, the place most closely associated with his name. According to legend he was miraculously transported over the waves in a stone boat coming to land near Killeany where he set about building one of the great influential monasteries of the age. The name Cill Éinne (Killeany) means, literally, The Church of Enda.

The remains of Enda's monastery are situated on the edge of An Trá Mór, the Big Strand, at the eastern end of Inishmore. All

Portions of a cross shaft which have been cemented together on the site of Enda's monastery. The intricate carving was typical of the high crosses of the period. The drawings show the design on both sides.

that remains today are two small stone churches, Teaghlach Éinne and Teampall Bheanáin, the stunt of a once lofty round tower and fragments of an inscribed stone cross. It is claimed that Enda's monastic 'city' extended from Teaghlach Éinne to Teampall Bheanáin. However these two surviving buildings probably stood apart from the main monastery, a fact that saved them from destruction when Cromwell's soldiers destroyed all of the other buildings to provide material for the fortification of Arkyne Castle near Killeany Harbour in the 17th century.

Teaghlach Éinne is situated in an ancient graveyard among the sandhills at the eastern end of An Trá Mór. This graveyard is reputed to be the burial place of Enda and over a hundred of his followers and it still serves as a cemetery for the people of the nearby villages.

Teampall Bheanáin overlooks the bay from a remarkable hilltop position. It is a tiny church, hardly fifteen feet in its internal length, and is constructed from massive stone slabs. Regarded as the smallest church in Europe, it is orientated from North to South in contrast with all the other Aran churches which are orientated East to West. Nearby are the ruins of a number of clochans, or beehive huts, and the remnant of a wall which may once have surrounded a cathair or monastic settlement.

The stump of a round tower can be seen in a field near the sheltered harbour. This tower is said to have been sixty metres high and to have been blown down in a storm in the late 17th century. Elaborately carved sections of the shaft of a cross, which were found near this site, stand in a field to the east of the tower.

Enda's monastery flourished for over five hundred years after the death of the saint. Many of the great saints of the early Irish church including Brendan the Navigator and Kieran of Clonmacnoise, studied there and monks from this foundation were to be found preaching the gospel in all parts of Europe during the Dark Ages. In the 11th century the monastery suffered a succession of disasters. It was almost destroyed by fire in 1020 A.D. and was raised by Vikings in 1017 A.D. and 1081 A.D. In time the community became apathetic and its rule lax until the arrival of Franciscan monks in the 15th century. The last recorded Abbot of Killeany died in 1400 A.D. but the monastery seems to have lived on, surviving the reign of Henry VIII when most of the Irish monasteries were suppressed, and to have continued its work until 1586 when it too was dissolved by his daughter Elizabeth I.

Many legends concerning miraculous events in the life of Enda are still related. One such story from the island's folklore concerns the visit of St. Colmcille to Killeany where he studied under Enda's discipline. Colmcille loved the peace and beauty of Aran and he asked Enda for a plot of ground on which he might build a cell. Enda refused feeling that Colmcille's fame would lead to his own name being forgotten. He feared that Aran would be known thereafter as Colmcille's island. Colmcille eventually persuaded Enda to allow him to take just as much land as his cloak would cover. When the cloak was spread on the ground it began to stretch and stretch. Enda snatched it up lest it cover the whole of his island. Colmcille became violently angry and he laid a curse on the island which was never to be lifted. He declared that strangers and foreigners would overrun the islands; that the land would not yield a harvest without great labour; that the cows would not produce milk in quantity; that turf would never be found there. Enda's greatest fear also came to pass for even today a greater devotion exists to St. Colmcille on the islands than to any other saint.

ONAGHT

The second greatest monastic settlement on Inishmore is known as the Seven Churches and it is found at Onaght in the western part of the island. It is unlikely that there ever were seven churches on this site for all that now remains are the substantial ruins of two churches and a number of domestic buildings. This monastery, like that at Killeany, occupies good land with a permanent supply of fresh water. A stream runs through the little valley where it is located and some of the deepest soil on Inishmore can be found there.

The older of the two churches dates from the 8th century and is dedicated to St. Brecan. When first built it was similar in size to Teaghlach Éinne but it was enlarged over the centuries and the west gable clearly shows the original dimensions. St. Brecan was renowned for his piety and for the severity of his rule but little is known of the details of his life. He is said to have been a monk in the Killeany community and to have succeeded Enda as Abbot but his reason for moving to Onaght remains a mystery.

Teampall A'Phoill, 'The Church of the Hollow' is situated a few metres further up the valley. It is a 15th century structure which was probably used as an ordinary parish church until relatively recent times. Located near these churches are remains of five rectangular domestic buildings. They date from various periods and some of them were built as late as the 16th century.

Within the monastic enclosure are a number of graves, regarded as the last resting place of Brendan and some of his monks. The site also contains several inscribed stones and a portion of the shaft of a cross.

* * *

Between the two major sites of Killeany and Onaght are the ruins of numerous other Early Christian structures. The most notable of these is Teampall an Ceathrar Alainn, 'The Church of the Four Comely Saints' situated south of the main road near the village of Cowrugh. The four saints mentioned in the dedication are Fursey, Brendan of Birr, Conall and Berchan. There are no records to explain why the church is dedicated to these saints nor do we know why they were described as An Ceathrar Alainn. South of this church, in a nearby field, is a holy well chosen by Synge as the supposed location of his play *The Well of the Saints.* A number of other churches are also found on Inishmore. Teampall MacDuach, dedicated to St. Colman a patron of sailors, and Teampall na Naomh, of which little is known, are both situated near the village of Kilmurvey. In the district of Mainistir, about one and a half kilometres west of Kilronan are Teampall Chiaráin, a church that originated in the Golden Age and was enlarged to its present substantial size in the Medieval period. This St. Chiaráin, a disciple of Enda's, is believed to be the founder of one of the greatest monasteries in Ireland — at Clonmacnoise. Some distance west of this is the much smaller Teampall Asurnai, thought to be dedicated to a female saint, Soarney, though this is in no way certain.

INISHMAAN

Inishmaan seems never to have supported a major monastic community though a complex of ruins exists on fertile land near the centre of the island, which indicates that a monastery may once have occupied the site. Teampall na Seacht mic Righ, of which only the foundations remain, commemorates seven brothers, of noble birth, who came here as hermits. Teampall Muire nearby, was a late medieval building which served as a parish

*Above – Teampall a'Phoill –
The Church of the Hollow. One
of the two churches at the
'Seven Churches' monastic site
on Inishmore. This 15th century
structure stands at the head of a
fertile well watered valley.
Nearby are the remains of
rectangular domestic buildings
from about the same period.*

*Left – Clochan na Carraige,
Inishmore, 1885, before restoration. This is a typical example of
a dry stone beehive hut. Such
clochan's were probably the
domestic dwellings in the Aran
monastic enclosure in the early
Christian period.*

church for over 500 years. Near the east shore of this island stands the well preserved remains of a small church known as Kilcanaragh, though the derivation of the name is not now known.

INISHEER

On Inisheer the remains of several churches can be seen though tradition maintains that others have been lost on the shifting sand dunes at the north end of the island. Some traces of the foundations of a church, Cill na Eacht nInion, the Church of the Seven Daughters, can be seen near the eastern side of the island. Nothing is known of these seven female saints but it is almost certain that they have no connection with the seven princes commemorated on Inishmaan.

Teampall Chaomháin, the Church of St. Cavan, is much better preserved. Like Teaghlach Éinne on Inishmore it stands in a graveyard among the sand dunes and is in constant danger of being covered completely by the movement of the sands. St. Cavan is believed to have been a brother of St. Kevin of Glendalough. A considerable devotion towards him still exists on Inisheer and 'Cavan' is a common Christian name for boys on the island. Teampall Ghobnait (or Kilgobnet, the Church of St. Gobnet), another small church, is dedicated to a female saint who is venerated in Munster and who found refuge for a time on Inisheer.

Left — Teampall Bheanáin — the tiny hilltop church dedicated to St. Benan. The walls are built of massive blocks of stone.

*Teampall MacDuach near Kilmurvey Inishmore is dedicated to
St. Colman MacDuach. The very fine medieval arch was part of an
extension in the Romanesque style.*

conQuest
of aran

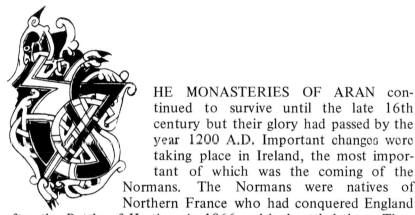

HE MONASTERIES OF ARAN continued to survive until the late 16th century but their glory had passed by the year 1200 A.D. Important changes were taking place in Ireland, the most important of which was the coming of the Normans. The Normans were natives of Northern France who had conquered England after the Battle of Hastings in 1066 and had settled there. They were soldiers and adventurers, skilled in warfare and highly organised under a single king. Ireland, by contrast, was a patchwork of tiny kingdoms ruled over in name only by a High King or Árd Rí. The Aran Islands were an almost independent territory ruled by the McTeige O'Briens, a branch of the powerful O'Brien family of Co. Clare.

Around the middle of the 12th century Dermot MacMurrough, King of Leinster was deprived of his territory after he had quarrelled with the Árd Rí and another Irish chieftain, O'Rourke of Breifne. Dermot fled to England where he recruited a band of Norman knights and footsoldiers. With this force he returned to Ireland in 1169 A.D. and rapidly conquered the fertile lands around the old Viking towns of Waterford, Wexford and Dublin. Dermot died leaving the Norman knights in possession of large tracts of land. Henry II, King of England, the overlord of the Normans, was crowned as King of Ireland.

The Norman's influence was largely confined to the east of the country and it was not until the 14th century that they attempted to subdue the wild and isolated west coast. The Lord Justice, one of the king's deputies, sailed up the west coast in 1334. Ancient records show that he plundered Inishmore, which, along with Inisheer had a considerable population at this time. It is thought that Inishmaan may have been uninhabited, except for a few monks or hermits.

The O'Brien's were allowed to continue as lords of the islands because the walled city of Galway had come to depend on their goodwill as masters of Galway Bay. The O'Brien's accepted an annual payment from the citizens for controlling piracy and for not interfering with trade to and from the city. This arrangement suited both parties and they tolerated one another in peace. The O'Brien's built a fortified tower house within the walls of Dun Formna. They may also have built a small castle at Killeany and they were the patrons of the Franciscan monastery established there in 1480. The mainland of Ireland was less peaceful than the islands during the 14th, 15th and 16th centuries with the Norman-English gradually increasing their influence. Certain branches of the Gaelic clans were prepared to recognise the English King as their overlord in order to gain control of the clan lands with his support. Such a conflict developed in 1584 among the O'Flaherty's of west Galway which resulted in the clan chief and his followers fleeing to Aran where they found refuge with the O'Brien's. The victorious branch of the clan, who had been supported by the English, pursued the fugitives and finally defeated them and their allies the O'Brien's. The Aran Islands passed into the hands of the O'Flaherty's. The reign of the O'Brien's was at an end, though they were to make repeated efforts to regain their lost lands.

The O'Brien's appealed to the Crown, and a Commission was established in Galway city in 1587 to decide on the ownership of the islands. The government, however, decided to annex the islands which they saw as being of strategic importance in the defence of the kingdom against French and Spanish enemies. They argued that the islands were monastery land and that, as the monasteries of Ireland and England had been suppressed by law and their lands taken over by the crown, the islands were the rightful property of the Queen. In the Government view neither the O'Briens or the O'Flahertys could be trusted and so the islands were granted to John Rawson of Athlone on condition that he kept the garrison of soldiers there. Thus the ownership of the land of Aran passed from those who lived on it and worked it. John Rawson, believed to have been the builder of Arkyne

Castle, sold the islands to the Lynch family of Galway in 1588.

Seventeenth century Ireland was a country ravaged by almost continuous warfare. By the middle of the century the battle lines were being drawn on a new basis, that of religion. Some of the native Irish chiefs and the Anglo-Norman lords, in 1642, united in the Confederation of Kilkenny, the aim of which was the restoration of the Catholic religion. Their opponent, Cromwell, the Lord Protector of England, landed in Dublin in 1649. He waged total war on his enemies, capturing the major towns and laying waste the countryside. Tens of thousands of civilians were given the option "to Hell or Connaught" and were driven westward by his victorious armies. The fertile lands which they vacated were given to planters from England and Scotland. It seems probable that some of the dispossessed who were forced to cross the Shannon into Connaught may have settled on the islands at this time.

The Marquis of Clanrickarde, one of the leaders on the Irish side, hoped that the tide could be turned if his French allies sent troops to Ireland as they had promised. He garrisoned the Aran Islands in order to preserve a point of entry for this expected aid. Sir Robert Lynch, the owner of the islands, was given the title of Commander-in-chief and he was supplied with 200 soldiers. Arkyne castle was fortified and Inishmore was placed on a war footing. The French force failed to arrive and the Irish were repeatedly defeated. Galway City fell to the Cromwellians in December 1650, though seven hundred officers and men from its garrison escaped to Inishboffin.

The small Aran garrison surrendered and a body of Cromwell's troops were sent to hold down the island and to strengthen Arkyne Castle. They demolished a number of ancient churches of St. Enda's monastery and used the stone as building material. While they were engaged on this work, in 1652, the Irish troops from Inishboffin took them by surprise and regained control of Arkyne. A Cromwellian force of 1300 men, under the command of General Reynolds laid siege to Arkyne. The garrison surrendered within a week and were allowed to take ship for the continent. Sir Robert Lynch was declared a traitor and his lands forfeit. The islands became the property of a Cromwellian, Erasmus Smith.

During the next decade the Government strengthened the defences of Arkyne Castle and made use of it as a prison camp for Catholic priests awaiting deportation to the West Indies. A

The 15th century O'Brien Castle at Inisheer.

garrison was maintained on the islands but in the more peaceful era of the 18th century the fortifications at Arkyne were allowed to crumble and the number of men stationed there dwindled. In the meantime the islands changed hands on several occasions. Erasmus Smith sold his interest to the Butler's of Ormond. Richard Butler received the title Earl of Aran in 1662 but this family soon parted with the land and those who later bore the title had no connection with Aran.

During the 18th and 19th centuries the islands were owned by a succession of absentee landlords whose sole interest was the income they received from rent. Agents, who were placed in charge, extracted huge rents from the island tenants whose living conditions worsened rapidly. By the early 19th century the tenants were paying over £2,000 per annum in rent to their land-lord, a huge sum in the values of the time, which must have severely strained the meagre resources of Aran.

The Fitzmaurice's of Galway City owned the islands for a time but lost them to the Digby family of Co. Kildare early in the 19th century on a mortgage which they failed to repay. In 1870 Elizabeth Digby married and became Countess of Howth and the ownership of Aran passed to her two surviving daughters, under her marriage settlement. Under the Land Acts of 1881 and 1882, tenants obtained the right to sell their interest in the land, and later were able to buy out their holdings under special purchase schemes. As a result, in the first two decades of the 20th century, most of the island families had acquired the ownership of their land.

A heavy load. A farmyard at Inishmaan.

THE OARSMEN'S SONG

It's only twice a week she comes
How we look forward to that day.
Like some good omen to our homes
She blows her note across the bay.
There's bread in chests and oil in drums,
A wardrobe and a mattress
A box of nibs, a card of combs,
And a mail bag full of letters.

As black and hollow as huge pods,
The currachs dandle on the wave,
Wild winch and pulley lower the goods,
The sailors shout, the seagulls rave.
There's whitewash brushes, bags of nails,
With bottled gas and liquor,
Long iron gates, enamel pails,
And a hamper made of wicker.

What we can't load we float behind —
Slim planks for rafters, boards for floors,
Back from the steamer to the land
We're lying heavy on the oars:
With tins of polish, panes of glass,
And shafts for scythes and shafts for spades,
A pram, a cot, a plastic bath,
And shaving soap and razor blades.

Seamus Heaney

aran in the 19th.century

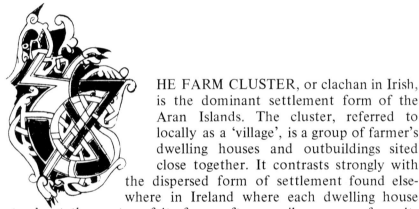

HE FARM CLUSTER, or clachan in Irish, is the dominant settlement form of the Aran Islands. The cluster, referred to locally as a 'village', is a group of farmer's dwelling houses and outbuildings sited close together. It contrasts strongly with the dispersed form of settlement found elsewhere in Ireland where each dwelling house stands at the centre of its farm, often a mile or more from its nearest neighbour. A typical clachan contains two to fifteen houses, irregularly grouped together without a main street, village green or market place. It usually does not have any services such as shop, pub, church or school though many of the Aran clachans have acquired one or more of these.

This type of settlement has deep roots in Irish history, going back almost to Celtic times. Like the great duns of Aran, each clachan housed a number of families, who held the surrounding land in common ownership. A fence enclosed a large tract of arable land known as the Infield where each individual farmer had a number of strips to grow crops. The unfenced pasture or rough grazing owned by the group was called the Outfield and each farmer was entitled to graze a number of animals on this.

Clachans were common in many parts of Ireland before the Great Famine of the 1840's. Thousands of people who were forced to move westwards into Connaught by Cromwell's armies in the seventeenth century settled in such groupings on the coasts of Galway and Mayo. Living close together gave the members of the group a sense of security and solidarity as they attempted to make a new life in a harsh environment. Some of the Aran 'villages' probably had their origins in this movement. After the famine, land holding was re-organised in the more fertile parts of Ireland and farm clusters were broken up in favour of isolated family dwellings, each of which stood on its own compact farm. On the west coast, however, the clachan remains though the communal ownership of land has almost totally disappeared.

Many clachans, and former clachans, in different parts of the country, contain the word "Bally" as an element in their place-names. "Bally" is derived from the Irish word "Baile" meaning a townland division and its cluster. The villages of Inishmaan almost all have names which include this element such as Ballintemple or Kimbally as do three of the four villages in Inisheer. Many of the Inishmore villages' names date from the monastic period, Killeany, Kilronan and Kilmurvey being examples, while others take their names from landscape features such as Sruthán, a stream, or Bungowla, the bottom of the fork.

The clachan type of settlement is a concrete expression of the close blood links and marriage links which exist on the Aran Islands. The surname Hernon embraces a majority of those living in Kilmurvey and Cooke is similarly associated with Bungowla and Gill with Killeany. Where related families live in close proximity to one another they are in a position to aid one another in their daily work or in a crisis. This giving of "cabhair" or help, often described as "cooring", depends not on the payment of money for work performed but rather on a return of the favour at the appropriate time. Tasks such as harvesting of rye or the burning of kelp, requiring a number of workers, can be carried out in this way. The giving and receiving of such aid is an important aspect of social organisation.

Almost all of the Aran clusters are found in the north, or leeside of the slopes. The exception, Gort na gCapall, is situated in the low neck of land between the two ridges of Inishmore where shelter is not available in any case. No dwelling houses are located on the crags at the back of the islands though a shed or barn can be seen in some isolated fields.

Other than in the case of Gort na gCapall the clusters are found on one of the two broad terraces midway between summit and shore. These broad terraces are backed by thick bands of shale and each is well watered by springs. The limited number of springs

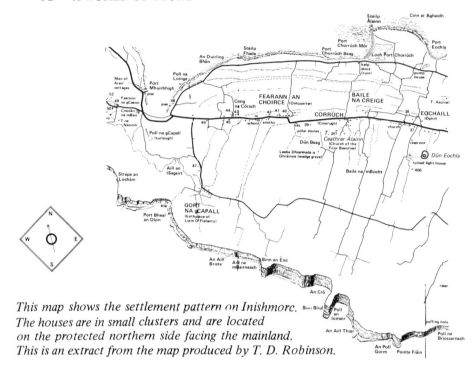

This map shows the settlement pattern on Inishmore.
The houses are in small clusters and are located
on the protected northern side facing the mainland.
This is an extract from the map produced by T. D. Robinson.

Where shore and land meet at Inisheer.

available is an added reason for the clustering of houses. Down-slope of the houses are the patches of arable land and pasture while upslope on the hilltops and the crags are the winter pastures. The carrying of water to the livestock in summer is an easy down-hill journey performed by the women while the men are busily engaged in fishing. The more difficult uphill journey in winter is regarded as a man's job.

In the pre-Famine period each Aran cluster consisted of 10 to 15 dwellings. The pattern of work moved up and down the slope with the seasons rather than along the slope. Thus the people living in a clachan were more concerned with the sea, the shore and the pasture and tillage below and the winter grazing above them than with the neighbouring clusters on the same terrace. The independence of each clachan is shown by the fact that the settlement of Iarairne was not even connected by road with the others, at the time the first detailed maps were completed in 1839. In the post-Famine period many of the clusters have shrunk, some, like Ballindun on Inishmaan, being reduced to two occupied houses. With the passage of time the individual clusters have been 'stretched' as new houses have been built along the road. Inish-maan, viewed from the sea, presents a continuous line of houses rather than a number of distinct villages. The number of 'villages' on Inishmore varies from ten to fourteen depending on whether one regards the smaller clusters as being independent of or merged with the larger.

On Aran settlement has tended to move downslope. New houses are generally taller than the old and their builders seek a lower more sheltered site. The ten houses in the 'village' of Sruthán on Inishmore were all sited above the road in pre-famine days but the whole village is now situated below the road. Killeany and Kilronan are larger than the other Aran settlements and have a wider range of functions than the traditional clachans. Killeany grew up around the 14th century Franciscan Friary and Arkyne Castle. Its sheltered harbour, protected by the castle, made it the 'capital' of the islands, and of West Connacht, for several centuries. The people of Killeany at that time were soldiers, sailors and government officials rather than farmers. They were divorced from the land as was the fishing community which grew up around the harbour. The castle and its garrison have long since gone but the people of Killeany are still less tied to the land than the other islanders. Kilronan resulted from the merging of two farm clusters along the main road early in the 19th century.

After the famine a newly built pier made it more important than Killeany. A courthouse, a police barracks and a coastguard station were sited there, giving it a completely different character to the other Inishmore clusters.

POPULATION

The population of Ireland increased rapidly during the second half of the eighteenth century. The country as a whole made little progress in industry or trade during this time. Farming was the only means of providing a living for this expanding population, especially on the isolated and underdeveloped west coast. Pressure on the land became more severe with each succeeding generation. The rule of primogeniture, that is inheritance by the first born, had never been observed in Ireland. A farmer would divide his land between all of his surviving children rather than pass it on to his eldest son and so, quite large farms were reduced to a collection of individually owned patches within a generation or two. The tenants who farmed such patches on Aran were rack-rented by their landlords. By the beginning of the 19th century the population of the islands had risen to 2,400; the vast majority of these had to eke out a living from a few rocky fields, while paying a total rental of over £2,000 per annum to an absentee landlord. This huge rent was often too great a burden on the tenants, who would fall into arrears. J. M. Synge witnessed the eviction of several Inishmaan farmers for non-payment of rent.

"Two recent attempts to carry out evictions on the island came to nothing, for each time a sudden storm rose, by, it is said, the power of a native witch, when the steamer was approaching, and made it impossible to land.

This morning, however, broke beneath a clear sky of June and when I came into the open air the sea and rocks were shining with wonderful brilliancy. Groups of men, dressed in their holiday clothes, were standing about, talking with anger and fear, yet showing a lurking satisfaction at the thought of the dramatic pageant that was to break the silence of the seas.

About half-past nine the steamer came in sight on the narrow line of sea-horizon that is seen in the centre of the bay, and immediately a last effort was made to hide the cows and sheep of the families that were most in debt.

Till this year no one on the island would consent to act as bailiff, so that it was impossible to identify the cattle of the

A typical Aran farm cluster of the late 19th century. The thatch roof cottages have small deep set windows. The stone walled fields are intensively tilled with 'lazy beds'.

defaulters. Now, however, a man of the name of Patrick has sold his honour, and the effort of concealment is practically futile.

This falling away from the ancient loyalty of the island has caused intense indignation and early yesterday morning, while I was dreaming on the Dun, this letter was nailed on the doorpost of the chapel:

'Patrick, the devil, a revolver is waiting for you. If you are missed with the first shot, there will be five more that will hit you.

'Any man that will talk with you, or work with you, or drink a pint of porter in your shop, will be done with the same way as yourself.'

As the steamer drew near I moved down with the men to watch the arrival, though no one went further than about a mile from the shore.

Two curaghs from Kilronan with a man who was to give help in identifying the cottages, the doctor, and the relieving officer, were drifting with the tide, unwilling to come to land without the support of the larger party. When the anchor had been thrown it gave me a strange throb of pain to see the boats being lowered, and the sunshine gleaming on the rifles and helmets of the constabulary who crowded into them.

Once on shore the men were formed in close marching order, a word was given, and the heavy rhythm of their boots came up over the rocks. We were collected in two straggling bands on either side of the roadway, and a few moments later the body of magnificent armed men passed close to us, followed by a low rabble, who had been brought to act as drivers for the sheriff.

After my weeks spent among primitive men this glimpse of the newer types of humanity was not reassuring. Yet these mechanical police, with the commonplace agents and sheriffs, and the rabble they had hired, represented aptly enough the civilization for which the homes of the island were to be desecrated.

A stop was made at one of the first cottages in the village, and the day's work began. Here, however, and at the next cottage, a compromise was made, as some relatives came up at the last moment and lent the money that was needed to gain a respite.

In another case a girl was ill in the house, so the doctor interposed, and the people were allowed to remain after a merely formal eviction. About midday, however, a house was reached where there was no pretext for mercy, and no money could be procured. At a sign from the sheriff the work of carrying out the

beds and utensils was begun in the middle of a crowd of natives who looked on in absolute silence, broken only by the wild imprecations of the woman of the house. She belonged to one of the most primitive families on the island, and she shook with uncontrollable fury as she saw the strange armed men who spoke a language she could not understand driving her from the hearth she had brooded on for thirty years. For these people the outrage to the hearth is the supreme catastrophe. They live here in a world of grey, where there are wild rains and mists every week in the year, and their warm chimney corners, filled with children and young girls, grow into the consciousness of each family in a way it is not easy to understand in more civilized places.

The outrage to a tomb in China probably gives no greater shock to the Chinese than the outrage to a hearth in Inishmaan gives to the people.

When the few trifles had been carried out, and the door blocked with stones, the old woman sat down by the threshold and covered her head with her shawl.

Five or six other women who lived close by sat down in a circle round her, with mute sympathy. Then the crowd moved on with the police to another cottage where the same scene was to take place, and left the group of desolate women sitting by the hovel.

There were still no clouds in the sky, and the heat was intense. The police when not in motion lay sweating and gasping under the walls with their tunics unbuttoned. They were not attractive, and I kept comparing them with the islandmen, who walked up and down as cool and fresh-looking as the sea-gulls.

When the last eviction had been carried out a division was made: half the party went off with the bailiff to search the inner plain of the island for the cattle that had been hidden in the morning, the other half remained on the village road to guard some pigs that had already been taken possession of.

After a while two of these pigs escaped from the drivers and began a wild race up and down the narrow road. The people shrieked and howled to increase their terror, and at last some of them became so excited that the police thought it time to interfere. They drew up in double line opposite the mouth of a blind laneway where the animals had been shut up. A moment later the shrieking began again in the west and the two pigs came in sight, rushing down the middle of the road with the drivers behind them.

They reached the line of the police. There was a slight scuffle, and then the pigs continued their mad rush to the east, leaving three policemen lying in the dust.

The satisfaction of the people was immense. They shrieked and hugged each other with delight, and it is likely that they will hand down these animals for generations in the tradition of the island.

Two hours later the other party returned, driving three lean cows before them, and a start was made for the slip. At the public-house the policemen were given a drink while the dense crowd that was following waited in the lane. The island bull happened to be in a field close by, and he became wildly excited at the sight of the cows and of the strangely dressed men. Two young islanders sidled up to me in a moment or two as I was resting on a wall, and one of them whispered in my ear:

'Do you think they could take fines of us if we let out the bull on them?'

In face of the crowd of women and children, I could only say it was probable, and they slunk off.

At the slip there was a good deal of bargaining, which ended in all the cattle being given back to their owners. It was plainly of no use to take them away, as they were worth nothing.

When the last policeman had embarked, an old woman came forward from the crowd and, mounting on a rock near the slip, began a fierce rhapsody in Gaelic, pointing at the bailiff and waving her withered arms with extraordinary rage.

'This man is my own son,' she said; 'it is I that ought to know him. He is the first ruffian in the whole big world.'

Then she gave an account of his life, coloured with a vindictive fury I cannot reproduce. As she went on the excitement became so intense I thought the man would be stoned before he could get back to his cottage.

On these islands the women live only for their children, and it is hard to estimate the power of the impulse that made this old woman stand out and curse her son.

In the fury of her speech I seem to look again into the strange reticent temperament of the islanders, and to feel the passionate spirit that expresses itself, at odd moments only, with magnificent words and gestures."

In such conditions the potato became the key to survival. It had been introduced into Ireland from the "New World" about the year 1600 A.D. It proved to be an ideal crop in the damp climate and produced good yields even from poor soils. It became the stable food of the people in the late 18th century and though a diet of potatoes and milk may have been monotonous it provided enough nourishment to sustain life. The sale of a calf or pig served to pay the rent and the farmer and his family subsisted on the produce of their potato patch. Fishermen and labourers who had not inherited land managed to sub-let a plot for a period of eleven months to grow a crop of potatoes. This practice was known as taking land on conacre.

A man who acquired land, through inheritance or rental, felt confident that he could support a family and so, tended to marry while still very young. The large families of such youthful marriages had increased the population of Aran to 3,521 by the year 1841. The islands, especially Inishmore, were overpopulated and the stage was set for disaster. Blight, a fungus that blackens the potato and renders it inedible struck the crop for the first time during the 1820's. It was to re-appear at regular intervals during the century leaving a trail of death and disease in its wake. The loss of the potato crop was the greatest disaster that could befall the hard pressed tenants.

The pressure which population exerted on resources in the late 19th century can be seen in the landscape of Inisheer, which was itself much less crowded than Inishmore.

In the following extract from Liam O'Flaherty's novel *Famine,* the Kilmartin family discover that potato blight is sweeping through their crop.

ANOTHER VIOLENT STORM CAME ON the last day of the month. They did not trouble greatly about this one, since the first had done no damage. Even so, a rumour got abroad that the blight had struck in the County Cork. Would it come this far? Every day, they anxiously inspected the crop. But the days passed without any sign of the evil. The potatoes that were dug for food still remained wholesome. It promised to be a miraculous crop. Even Mary began to take courage. And then, on the fifteenth of July, the bolt fell from the heavens.

When old Kilmartin came into his yard shortly after dawn on that day, he looked up the Valley and saw a white cloud standing above the Black Lake. It was like a great mound of snow, hanging by an invisible chain, above the mountain peaks. It was dazzling white in the glare of the rising sun.

"Merciful God!" he said. "What can that be?"

The rest of the sky was as clear as crystal. The old man stared at it in awe for some time. Then he ran into the house and called out the family to look at it. Mary and Thomsy came out. They were as startled as the old man.

"Did you ever see anything like that?" the old man said.

"Never in my natural," said Thomsy. "It's like a....."

"Snow," Mary said. "It's like a big heap of snow."

"How could it be snow?" said the old man. "And this the middle of summer? It's a miracle."

"Or would it be a bad sign. God between us and harm?" said Thomsy.

Other people came from their cabins and stared at the cloud. There was a peculiar silence in the Valley. The air was as heavy as a drug. There was not a breath of wind. The birds did not sing. And then, as the people watched, the cloud began to move lazily down upon the Valley. It spread out on either side, lost its form and polluted the atmosphere which became full of a whitish vapour, through which the sun's rays glistened; so that it seemed that a fine rain of tiny whitish particles of dust was gently falling from the sky. Gradually a sulphurous stench affected the senses of those who watched. It was like the smell of foul water in a sewer. Yet, there was no moisture and the stench left an aris feeling in the nostrils. Even the animals were affected by it. Dogs sat up on their haunches and howled. Not a bird was to be seen, although there had been flocks of crows and starlings about on the previous day. Then, indeed, terror seized the people and a loud wailing broke out from the cabins, as the cloud overspread the whole Valley, shutting out the sun completely.

All this time, the whole Kilmartin family had remained in the yard. Mary clutched the baby in her arms. Nobody thought of preparing breakfast, although the morning was now well advanced. It was only when the wailing began and Maggie joined in it, that Mary came to her senses and said:

"Don't frighten the child with your whining. There's no harm done yet. Hold the baby, mother, while I get breakfast ready."

"True for you," said the old man. "There's no harm done yet. Into the house, all of you. Pooh! Afraid of a fog, is it?" Maggie stopped crying, but she went back to bed and closed the door of her room. The others made an attempt to be cheerful. Like people who feel the oncoming panic of despair, they gave voice to expressions of optimism, which they knew to be false.

"I often saw fogs heavier than that," Ellen Gleeson said, as she rocked the baby in the hearth corner.

"As heavy as that?" said Thomsy. "Sure that's not a heavy fog. I saw a fog once that was as thick as night. You can see to the end of the yard in this one."

"You can see farther," said the old man. "On the south side there, you can see as far as Patsy O'Hanlon's house. It's not a thick fog. It's funny the smell that comes from fogs."

"I never smelt a fog before like that," said Mary. "It must be a new kind of fog. But a fog can do no harm in any case. If it was rain now, that would be a different story. Rain might rot the potatoes and they..."

"Nothing will rot the potatoes," said the old man. "God forgive you for saying such a thing."

Mary cooked some Indian meal and turnips, of which a few still remained. While they were eating, a further astonishing thing happened. The sky cleared almost instantaneously. The sun shone brilliantly. Yet this change, which should have cheered the watchers, only increased their awe, for the stench still remained. They all stopped eating. The old man got to his feet. He reached for his hat and fumbled with it, looking about him at the others with the expression of a small boy who has committed some offence of which he is ashamed.

"Blood an ouns!" Thomsy said, jumping to his feet.

With his mouth wide open, he stared at the old man. Then they both clapped their hats on their heads and rushed from the house. Mary ran to the cradle, picked up the child and pressed it to her bosom.

"What ails ye?" her mother said.

Maggie began to wail in the bedroom. All the colour had gone from Mary's cheeks and her eyes seemed to have enlarged. She handed the baby to her mother and whispered:

"I'm going out to look at the gardens."

Thomsy and the old man, one after the other and with their hands behind their backs, were walking slowly down towards the potato gardens, still shining in all the glory of their dark-green foliage, under the radiant sun. But the stench was now terrible. In single file, they came to the first garden and leaned over the stone fence close together, staring at the plants.

Uttering shriek after shriek, he climbed over the fence, fumbling so much that he dislodged several stones. He strode through the stalks, that came up to his waist, across the ridges, until he came to the affected spot. The stench was now that of active corruption. The old man seized the stalks that were marked with spots and began to pull them. The leaves withered when he touched them and the stalks snapped like rotten wood. But the potatoes clinging to the uprooted stalks were whole. The old man dug into several of them with his nails.

"They're not rotten," he cried, laughing hysterically. "Come on, Thomsy. Pull the stalks that are rotten. We must stop it spreading."

Excited by the old man's frenzy, Thomsy also climbed over the fence and waddled through the stalks, but he halted when he was a few yards from the old man who was pulling feverishly and shouting. The old man was now surrounded by a widening lake of spots.

"Sure, it's flying all over the garden," said Thomsy. "Look, man. It's all round you. You can't stop it."

"What's that?" said the old man, raising his head.

He looked all round him pathetically. Then his mouth fell open and he stood up straight. His hands dropped to his sides.

"You're right," he said faintly. "It's the hand of God. God's will be done."

Thereupon he crossed himself and bowed his head. Not troubling even to collect the potatoes he had pulled up with the stalks, he marched slowly back to the fence, carelessly trampling over the stalks that were still untouched. Mary turned away from the fence as he approached. She began to walk back to the house.

The wailing was now general all over the Valley.

"They're alright," said the old man. "There's nothing on them."

"Whist!" said Thomsy. "What's that I hear?"

Towards the north, in the direction towards which Thomsy pointed, Mary and the old man saw people looking over fences, just as they themselves were doing. These people had begun to wail. In this wailing there was a note of utter despair. There was no anger in it, no power, not even an appeal for mercy. It was just like the death groan of a mortally wounded person, groaning in horror of inevitable death.

"It's the blight," Mary whispered. "Oh! God in Heaven!"

"Look," gasped the old man through his teeth. "Look at it. It's the devil. It's the devil himself."

With outstretched hand, that trembled as if palsied, he pointed to a little hollow about ten yards within the fence. Here the growth was particularly luxuriant and the branches of the potato stalks were matted as thickly as a carpet. Mary and Thomsy followed the direction of his hand and while he babbled foolishly they saw the evil appear on the leaves. A group of little brown spots had appeared and they spread, as if by magic, while they watched. It was just like the movement of an incoming tide over a flat, sandy shore. It was a rain of spots, spreading rapidly in all directions. "Oh! God Almighty!" Thomsy cried. "Save us, oh, Lord! Jesus! Mary and Joseph!"

Cormorants, Inishmore.

The Famine, more correctly the Great Hunger, of the 1840's brought catastrophe on the country as a whole. Blight, aided by bad weather, completely destroyed the crop in 1845, 1846 and 1847. One million people died of hunger and famine fever and a million others fled the country, emigrating to the industrial cities of England and Scotland, and especially, to the United States.

The Aran Islands, and the west coast in general, seem to have escaped the worst effects of the disaster. The population of Inishmore decreased but the percentage decline was far less than the national average. The number of people living on Inishmaan and Inisheer actually increased during the decade. These islands were less crowded than Inishmore and they may even have provided refuge for people from the mainland. The availability of food from the sea and the shore blunted the effects of crop failure on all three islands.

POPULATION FIGURES

Year	Inisheer	Inishmaan	Inishmore	Total
1812				2,400
1821	421	387	2,285	3,093
1831				3,191
1841	456	473	2,592	3,521
1851	518	503	2,312	3,333
1861	532	478	2,289	3,299
1871	495	433	2,122	3,050
1881	497	473	2,193	3,163
1891	455	456	1,996	2,907
1901	483	421	1,959	2,863

Aran was not to fare so well during the remainder of the century. Partial failures of the potato crop occurred on the west coast in 1879 and 1889 causing great suffering and hardship once more. The morale of the people could not withstand such repeated blows. Emigration, a trickle since the 1820's and a steady stream since the 1840's, now became a flood as the young departed in search of a more promising life abroad. The community lost confidence in its own ability to survive. Farmers tried to keep their farms intact to pass on to one son when the others would all have departed. Men were slow to enter into marriage waiting cautiously until they would have the security of ownership before taking a partner. Many waited too long and failed to marry at all.

Name and Description of Parishes, &c.	Inhabited Houses.	By how many Families occupied.	Houses now building	Families chiefly employed in Agriculture	Families chiefly employed in Trade. Manufactures & Handic.	All other Families not comprised in the two preceding classes	Males.	Females,
The three Islands of Arran, Half Barony and Parish of Arran, viz.								
Island of Eniseer,	47	47	4	46	-	1	141	154
Island of Enismane,	51	55	3	51	4	-	164	156
Killeany Village in Great Island	78	82	2	78	4	-	249	211
Kilronan, ditto,	52	52	2	48	4	-	191	169
Manister, ditto,	9	9	1	9	-	-	26	25
Oghill, ditto,	24	24	-	20	3	1	64	54
Ballinacreggy, ditto,	22	22	2	19	3	-	67	63
Oat-quarter, ditto,	19	19	-	17	2	-	60	45
Gorthnagapple ditto,	18	18	1	18	-	-	49	53
Kilmurry, ditto,	15	15	-	15	-	-	43	50
Corrig, ditto,	10	10	-	10	-	-	28	38
Onaught, ditto,	19	19	1	19	-	-	59	51
Cregaherean, ditto,	20	20	-	20	-	-	64	63
Bungowley, ditto,	11	11	-	11	-	-	39	24
Total,	395	400	17	381	20	2	1244	1156

Census of the Aran Islands 1812.

The burial memorials, found in groups, along the roadways of Inishmore, remain a mystery to scholars. The inscriptions which commemorate individuals, date from the late 18th and early 19th centuries but it is believed that mounds of stones existed on these sites long before the monuments were cemented and decorated with crosses and plaques in the early 19th century.

As each succeeding generation of young people left, the islands developed a society of aged spinsters and bachelors.

Inishmore has suffered most in the general decline. The villages of Killeany and Kilronan contributed largely to this and their inhabitants depended on the fishing industry which slumped disastrously in the late 19th century. The other islands fared better, probably because they have always had a more equal balance between their populations and available resources.

THE IRISH LANGUAGE

By the year 1800 A.D. the Irish language was being abandoned as the vernacular, or daily spoken language, of the majority of Irish men. English was spoken in the homes of the prosperous and Irish was regarded as the language of the poor and the backward. The number of Irish speakers did increase in the country as a whole between the years 1800 and 1840 but only because the population, particularly the poorer sections, increased rapidly during this period. The repeated famines after 1840 affected the poor more than any other class and so dealt a death blow to their language. From 1870 onwards the rate of emigration from the Irish speaking counties of the west was far higher than the national average.

By 1891, eighty-five percent of Irishmen spoke English only and though fourteen percent spoke both English and Irish, only one percent of the total population relied on Irish as their sole means of communication. The Aran islands were among the few areas in the country to retain their native language in daily use throughout the course of the 19th century. The pressures to abandon the language were many. The business of the State, carried on in Aran by the police, the courts and the coastguards, was   conducted only through English. Those who held salaried positions and lived a secure and comfortable lifestyle were all seen to be speakers of English. The National Education Acts of 1831 brought primary education to the islands in the second half of the century. The national schools ignored the language of the children's homes and did their best to create a generation of English speakers. Education brought the possibility of clerical and teaching jobs for some island children, jobs which demanded a knowledge of English rather than of Irish. Contact with the outside world increased decade by decade and English speaking scholars and tourists began to visit the islands to study the monasteries and duns. Most important of all, the majority of the young knew they would have to emigrate in search of a living. They would have to enter into, and seek to prosper in, an English speaking world in Britain or the United States. Though many emigrants preserved their language among their family and kin groups, in their new homes they had to equip themselves with the language of their workmates and neighbours. The Irish language was seen as a bar to successful emigration.

There was no awareness in the London-based Government or indeed among native Irish politicians that the preservation of the language was a matter of importance. The great political issues of Catholic Emancipation, Home Rule and the Land League were discussed and campaigned for through the English language. In 1891 the Congested Districts Board was set up in an effort to improve the economy of the poorer areas of the west. This Board certainly helped the islanders in their battle for survival but it too did not attach any importance to the preservation of the language.

All of these pressures were not without some result, even on Aran. The use of Irish declined on Inishmore, particularly in the vicinity of Kilronan where the forces in favour of English were most evident. Inisheer also suffered a decline, due in part to the presence there of a coastguard unit and to its nearness to the Co. Clare mainland where the language was rapidly losing ground. Only on the most isolated of the islands, Inishmaan did there remain a majority of people who were unable to speak English. Even here, the introduction of a national school resulted in some weakening of the position of Irish.

Isolation was a major factor in preserving the language on Aran. Even within the islands Irish fared best in those places which were furthest from the centres of administration and trade. But a review of the events of the 19th century in Ireland, and particularly in Aran, reveals an undeniable fact which is that a language cannot survive when the society which speaks that language is being destroyed and the people who learned it from the cradle are being forced to emigrate.

THE CONGESTED DISTRICTS BOARD

A century of hunger, disease, eviction and emigration finally aroused the conscience of the then Government, which set up the Congested Districts Board in 1891 in an attempt to improve social and economic conditions in the poorest parts of the country. A district was regarded as congested if the rateable valuation was less than 30/- (£1.50) per head of the population. The Congested Districts, then, were areas where each family did not have sufficient land to provide anything other than a very low standard of living. Almost all of the west coast, including the Aran Islands, was badly congested according to this definition.

The Congested Districts Board attempted to enlarge holdings where land could be bought or reclaimed. They encouraged domestic industries such as the knitting of sweaters and they sought to improve fishing by building piers and by providing nets and boats. There was no land available on Aran for redistribution but the Board met with some success in their efforts to encourage craftwork and fishing.

Before commencing work in each area the Board's inspectors made an inquiry into local conditions using a number of standard questions. These 'Base Line' reports are a reliable and accurate record of life in the Congested Districts. The report on the Aran Islands, which follows, gives a detailed picture of social and economic conditions on the islands at that time.

Confidential.

CONGESTED DISTRICTS BOARD FOR IRELAND.

COUNTY OF GALWAY—UNION OF GALWAY.

REPORT OF MAJOR RUTTLEDGE-FAIR, *Inspector.*

DISTRICT

OF

ARAN ISLANDS.

No. .

STATISTICAL TABLE.

Electoral Division.	Area in Statute Acres.	Poor Law Valuation.	Number of Ratings at and under £10 and above £4 Valuation.	Number of Ratings at and under £4 Valuation.	Population in 1891.	Number of Families in 1891.	Number of Families on Holdings exceeding £2 and under £4 Valuation.	Number of Families on Holdings at and under £2 Valuation.	Number of Families in very poor circumstances.	Number of Families which have no Cattle.
		£								
Inishmore,	11,288	1,576	117	578	2,907	562	186	279	60	30
Totals,	11,288	£1,576	117	578	2,907	562	186	279	60	30

(1.) Whether inland or maritime.

This district comprises a group of five inhabited islands at the entrance to Galway Bay; Inishmore or North Island, Inishmaan or Middle Island, Inisheer or South Island, and Straw and Rock Islands; the only people on the last two islands are lighthouse keepers and their families. Inishmore is by far the largest and most thickly populated, having nearly 2,000 inhabitants.

(2.) Average quantity of land cultivated on holdings at and under £4 valuation, under (*a*) oats, (*b*) potatoes, (*c*) meadow, (*d*) green crops.

There are on an average about one and three-quarter acres cultivated on holdings at and under £4 valuation, in the following way :—

Potatoes,	.	.	.	$1\frac{1}{4}$ Acres.
Barley or Rye,	.	.	.	$\frac{1}{4}$,,
Meadow,	.	.	.	$\frac{1}{4}$,,
			Total,	$1\frac{3}{4}$ Acres.

A few perches of cabbages are also sown.

(3.) Extent of mountain or moor grazing, and rights possessed by tenants, whether in common or otherwise.

There is no mountain or moor grazing in this district.

(4.) Extent and description of land, if any, which could be profitably reclaimed and added to existing adjoining holdings.

There is no land in this district which could be profitably reclaimed and added to existing adjoining holdings.

(5.) Particulars as to any suitable land in the district which could be obtained, and to which families could be migrated with a reasonable prospect of success.

There is no suitable land in this district which could be obtained, and to which families could be migrated with a reasonable prospect of success.

(6.) Method of cultivation, manures, rotation of crops, etc., etc.

No rotation of crops is followed in this district, the amount of land suitable for tillage being quite insufficient for such a purpose. Potatoes are the chief crop and are sown year after year in the same plots ; about a rood of barley or rye, and in some instances, though rarely, oats is also sown. The soil being of a sandy nature is not suitable for growing oats. Sea-weed is the principal manure, thousands of tons of the best weed being washed ashore in stormy weather. As live stock are not housed during the winter months there is no farm-yard manure available.

(7.) General information with regard to stock, and suggestions as to improvement of breeds—(a) cattle, (b) sheep, (c) horses and donkeys, (d) pigs, (e) poultry, etc., etc.

The islanders possess a good breed of both cattle and sheep, the former being bred from good Shorthorn bulls imported from County Clare, and the latter crossed with rams bred in that County also. The Aran cattle always bring the highest price at the neighbouring fairs and markets on the mainland. The islanders are most anxious to secure a few well-bred Shorthorn bulls, and applications are about to be made to the Board for assistance. The usual fee charged for the bull's services is from 5s. to 7s., a much higher sum than is customary on the mainland. The islanders, however, do not object to such charges as it is well known bulls could not otherwise be profitably kept.

There are a number of fairly good mares on the North Island, but the sires are a very poor lot. A good Hackney stallion would, I think, be suitable to cross with the island mares, or better still, a Barb sire.

Pigs.—These are generally purchased on the mainland, sows not being kept.

Poultry—These are deteriorating ; if a few sittings of eggs could be distributed through the islands, among reliable persons, an improvement might be easily effected.

(8.) Markets and fairs for cattle and produce of district; also statement as to where the people obtain food and other supplies, and the prevailing custom with regard to the disposal of butter, eggs, and poultry ; to what extent they are sold in the first instance to local shopmen and dealers ; and generally speaking, how old the eggs are when sold to the first buyer, and about how old when they reach their ultimate destination in Great Britain.

Buyers from County Clare generally visit the islands in the spring and summer months to purchase live stock, and most of the cattle and sheep are sold to them. Any not disposed of in this way are taken to Galway and Spiddal fairs where they are eagerly sought after owing to their superior breed and fattening qualities. All supplies such as food, &c., are obtained at Galway. The number of eggs disposed of is insignificant as compared with other districts, though the people seem to have a number of fowls.

(9.) Rail, steamer, sailing boat, road, postal and telegraph facilities.

All communications are now carried on by steamer with Galway and a telegraph office has recently been opened at Kilronan.

The steamer only calls once a week at the Middle and South Islands.

(10.) Employment for labourers in district, whether temporary or constant, and rate of wage.

There is scarcely any employment for labourers in this district; except in spring and summer. The rate of wage is 1s. 6d. per day and food.

(11.) Migratory labour, average earnings per head, and where earned.

There are no migratory labourers in this district.

(12.) Weaving, spinning, knitting, and sewing, whether used locally or sold, and where.

It is said that more weaving, knitting, &c., was carried on formerly, as almost all the islanders, both young and old, then wore flannel ; now the young people purchase considerable quantities of tweeds and other shop goods. Still flannel and frieze are a great deal worn, particularly by the Middle and South Islanders. Nothing woven or spun is ever sold, as far as I can learn.

(13.) Kelp-burning, and sale of sea-weed.

More than two-thirds of the people burn kelp, and it is estimated that on an average each family makes at least two tons. The average price is now quite £4 per ton, showing that nearly £1,500 is paid for kelp in this district. Trade for the last two years has been very brisk, and any quantity of good kelp can be sold at very remunerative prices.

There is no turf on these islands.

Lobster fishing is not carried on to any appreciable extent by the Aran islanders, though the Connemara fishermen catch numbers of lobsters in the immediate vicinity.

Sea fishing may be divided into three periods ; from December to April for cod and ling ; from April to end of June, Spring mackerel ; August to November, herring and Autumn mackerel. Cod and ling fishing is carried on at present in small canvas-covered canoes or curraghs manned by three men. These boats, though very suitable in any reasonable weather for crossing from island to island, are not safe for fishing purposes, especially during the winter season, and much time is lost in enforced idleness when the weather is at all unfavourable.

To develop this fishing, larger and better manned boats are required.

The facilities for the sale of fish are now very good, especially during the Spring mackerel fishing, but the people of the South Island, who are nine miles from Kilronan, are very anxious that the steamer should call twice instead of once a week, so as to enable them to dispose of their fish more readily.

There are 116 curraghs, twelve small sailing boats, third class, and four large trading boats in this district employed in fishing, or carrying turf or sea-weed.

Cod and ling are sold to local buyers, who dispose of them in Galway.

Cod and ling are salted in a very rough way ; otherwise fish-curing is unknown.

There are four piers on the islands—three on the North, Kilmurvey, Kilronan, and Killeany, and one on the Middle Island. None of these piers are accessible at low water, and in other respects, too, they are very faulty. The pier at Kilmurvey is seriously damaged, and, unless repaired, will probably be swept away by the next north-east storm. It is a useful structure, and should not be allowed to remain in its present state. A comparatively small sum would repair the existing breach, and for about £500 additional, an extension of about forty feet towards deep water could be effected.

The pier at Kilronan is the most availed of, but it was wrongly placed, and at low water is inaccessible even for small hookers. It is evident if the Spring mackerel fishing continues to be worked from Kilronan that a pier at which boats can come alongside at any state of the tide for shelter, as well as for convenience, should be provided. The bay is much exposed to north-east gales, and should a storm spring up suddenly, as often occurs on the West Coast, the fishing fleet would be placed in a very perilous condition, under existing circumstances.

It has been proposed either to extend the present pier or build a new one. So far as I can judge an extension of the present pier would not effectively remedy the defects which now exist, as there is no great depth of water south-west of the present pier, and an extension therefore in that direction does not seem sufficient to warrant the expenditure required. The alternative scheme, viz., to build a new pier, is one which though involving a large outlay, probably at least seven or eight thousand pounds, would undoubtedly give the required facilities. The proposed site is about 150 yards east of the existing pier and close to deep water at all states of the tide.

The pier at Killeany, though the most sheltered on the islands, is not accessible to large boats except at high water; I do not see how it could be improved.

On the Middle Island a pier built by the Board of Works is useful for landing turf, &c., &c., but it is too much exposed to allow boats to be kept there, neither can it be approached in bad weather.

I was shown a little cove on the south side of the Middle Island where the fishermen launch their curraghs from a rocky terrace which might be considerably improved by cutting away some projecting rocks and filling the cavities and fissures with concrete; a pier could not be attempted, but a small expenditure would make the place much more accessible for curraghs.

As regards the South Island, landing at any place in unsettled weather is both difficult and dangerous, and there is no place sufficiently sheltered that a pier which could be of any real use could be erected. A proposal has been put forward to make a harbour on this island by connecting Lough More with the sea. This lake covers an area of thirteen statute acres, and has a great depth of water, as much as ninety feet in places. It is situated at the east side of the island less than 300 yards from low water mark. The cutting through which boats would pass is not a long one, and if an entrance could once be made, boats of the largest size would be perfectly safe in any weather, and an invaluable harbour would be secured. The proposal is one worthy of very careful consideration, and in any event a survey should be made to determine the cost of the proposed works.

There are no salmon or freshwater fisheries in this district.

There are neither Banks nor Loan Funds in this district.

There are no mineral or other resources in this district.

Long credit is not now given; as a rule from three to six months to reliable customers is generally allowed. Shop-keepers' charge from twenty to twenty-five per cent. on all goods sold on credit. Considerable barter is carried on in fish, which are exchanged for sugar, flour, and tea, especially in the well-known village of Killeany.

The estimated *cash* receipts and expenditure of a family in ordinary circumstances, are as follow :—

RECEIPTS.	£	s.	d.	EXPENDITURE.	£	s.	d.
Sale of 5 pigs,	10	0	0	Rent,	3	0	0
„ cattle,	7	0	0	Clerical dues,	0	10	0
„ sheep,	5	0	0	Clothes,	6	0	0
„ 1 foal,	5	0	0	Meal and flour,	12	0	0
„ kelp,	9	0	0	Groceries,	6	11	0
„ eggs,	1	0	0	Tobacco,	2	12	0
„ butter, wool, and seaweed,	2	0	0	Spades,	0	10	0
„ fish,	3	0	0	Extras,	2	0	0
				Turf,	3	4	0
	£42	0	0		£36	7	0

The estimated *cash* receipts and expenditure of a family in poor circumstances are as follow :—

RECEIPTS.	£	s.	d.	EXPENDITURE.	£	s.	d.
Sale of 2 pigs,	4	0	0	Rent,	1	10	0
„ sheep,	2	0	0	Clerical dues,	0	5	0
„ fish,	4	0	0	Clothes,	5	0	0
„ 1 calf,	4	0	0	Meal and flour,	9	0	0
„ kelp,	9	0	0	Groceries,	3	10	0
„ seaweed,	1	0	0	Tobacco,	2	12	0
„ eggs,	1	0	0	Turf,	3	4	0
				Extras,	1	0	0
	£25	0	0		£26	1	0

(26.) Estimated value of home-grown food consumed, and period during which it lasts.

In good seasons potatoes generally last till the new crop is available, in the month of June. The value of home-grown food, consisting almost entirely of potatoes, may be estimated at from £12 to £15.

(27.) Dietary of people — number of meals daily, and kinds of food throughout the year.

The dietary of the people of this district consists of potatoes, flour, tea, sugar, and fish. Three meals are taken daily ; one in the morning about nine o'clock, the second about one o'clock, and the evening meal between seven and eight o'clock. Meat is rarely used except on festive occasions, such as Christmas and Easter.

(28.) Clothing — whether home made or bought, etc., etc.

For my remarks upon the clothing of the people of this district, see paragraph 12 of this report.

(29.) Dwellings : kind of houses, home-life and customs, etc., etc.

The houses in this district are, as a rule, substantially built thatched cottages, containing three rooms, a kitchen, and two sleeping apartments, and except in the case of very poor people, they are fairly well furnished. In every respect, particularly as regards cleanliness, they are far superior to the houses occupied by the Connemara peasantry.

(30.) Character of the people for industry, etc., etc.

The people of the district are fairly industrious and hard-working, and may, I think, be depended upon to take advantage of any opportunity that may be afforded to improve their circumstances. Like most of the islanders on the West Coast they are very suspicious.

(31.) Whether any organized effort has been made to develop the resources or improve the condition of the people. If so, by what means.

I am not aware of any organized effort having been made to develop the resources, or improve the condition of the people of this district.

(32.) Suggestions as to any possible method for improving the condition of the people in future.

It is evident that for islands so situated fishing should be the main resource of the people, yet owing to causes which the Board no doubt realise the islanders hitherto could not be considered fishermen. In only one village on the thickly populated North Island, and on the South Island, was fishing carried on to any appreciable extent.

The efforts recently made by the Board to provide a market and render the transit of fish comparatively easy have already borne fruit, and there is an eagerness now apparent amongst a considerable number of the people to apply themselves energetically to improving their condition by fishing. To thoroughly develop that industry at Aran it is most necessary that one or two places where boats can always be placed in safety and be able to proceed to sea in all weathers suitable for fishing should be provided, and I would therefore specially direct the attention of the Board to my suggestions in paragraph 20. The resources of the people might also be improved by the development of market gardening, an industry for which Aran, owing to the mildness of its climate during the winter and early spring months, is especially suitable.

Hitherto the difficulties of transport were an effectual barrier against any effort in this direction, but now the services of a steamer are available three times a week for the conveyance of produce to Galway where a market would soon be found. Further, the Arklow and other fishermen, who now make Aran their headquarters, are most anxious to purchase vegetables if they could be obtained, and have constantly told me they would be willing to give the highest price for them.

I think premiums for the best plots of early potatoes, white turnips, cabbages, &c., &c., should be offered by the Board, and if this course was adopted the industry would probably get a fair start.

Early in February I saw at the Aran Coast-guard Station potatoes over ground, which had been sown shortly before Christmas.

31st March, 1893.

ROBERT RUTTLEDGE-FAIR,
Inspector.

Dún Eochla dominates the Eastern end of Inishmore from its hill top position. Nearby are the remains of the lighthouse built in the early 19th century but later abandoned. The limestone pavement in the foreground, strewn with loose rocks and criss-crossed by fissures, is devoid of vegetation.

place names of aran

All these places are marked on the map, pages 8 and 9

INISHMORE / INIS MÓR
(The Big Island)

Arkyne's Castle
A castle built near Killeany by the O'Briens. Later it was rebuilt by Cromwellian soldiers, using stones from St. Enda's monastery.

Baile na m'Bocht
The remains of a stone wall found here may once have been part of the walls of a dun.

Brannock Island /
Oileán dá Bhranóg
The Irish means "the island of the two little ravens". It is situated west of Inishmore.

Bun Gowla / Bun Gabhla
"The bottom of the fork" — it is the westernmost village on the island.

Cowrugh / Corrúch
A village on the road between Kilronan and Kilmurvey.

Dún Aengus / Dún Aonghasa
"Aengus Fort" — it is said that Aengus was one of the chiefs of the Fir Bolg. Dún Aengus is built on the edge of a high cliff overlooking the Atlantic.

Dún Dúchathair
"The Black Fort" Cathair is another name for a stone fort. Dún Dúchathair is a promontory fort, on the south west of the island.

Dún Eochla
"The Fort of the Yew Wood". Dún Eochla is built near the highest point on Inishmore. Its site was later chosen for the building of a lighthouse.

Dún Eonaghta
"The Fort of the Eonaght Family". They are said to have been a Munster clan who once ruled Aran. Dún Eonaghta is built on good land.

Glassan Rock
The south eastern point of the island, from which fishing for 'wrasse' takes place.

Gort na gCapall

"The Field of the Horses". This is the only village on the western seaboard of the island. Liam O'Flaherty the author was born here.

Iarairne

Possible means "The Back of the Island". Locally it is known as The Dog's Head because of its shape.

Killeany / Cill Éinne

The Irish means St. Enda's Church. St. Enda built his monastery here. It is the second largest village on the island and once was quite a busy fishing port.

Kilmurvey / Cill Mhuirbhigh

The Irish means "the Church near the sandy beach". Quite a good road runs from Kilronan to the village of Kilmurvey.

Kilronan / Cill Rónáin

The Irish means St. Ronan's Church. It is the largest village on the Aran Islands. Its harbour, built with the help of the Congested District s Board, is large enough for the steamer from Galway. Most of the goods – foodstuffs, building materials, fuel etc. – imported to the islands are delivered to Kilronan, and then collected by their owners.

Loch Port Charrugh

A lagoon cut off from the sea, on the north of the island.

Mainistir

A village west of Kilronan.

Oghil / Eochaill

Eochaill is a townland not far from Kilronan.

Onaght / Eoghanacht

A townland near the site of the Seven Churches Monastery. Birthplace of M. O'Direain.

Poll na bPéist

"The Serpent's Hole". This is one of the most spectacular puffing holes on the island.

Poll na Brioscharnach

A sea arch on the south of the island.

Poll na gCapall

A turloch (an impermanent lake) located east of Kilmurvey.

Port Murvey / Port Mhuirbhigh

A village situated at the narrow neck of the island.

Rock Island / An t'Oileán Iarthach

An island west of Inishmore. A lighthouse was erected here in the mid-nineteenth century.

Sruthan

Located between Kilmurvey and Onaght where an intermittent stream is found.

Straw Island / Oileán na Tuí

A small island off the south-east coast of Inishmore. In times past rye was grown here for thatching.

Teaghlach Éinne

"St. Enda's House". One of the only buildings remaining from St. Enda's monastery.

Teampall a'Phoill

"The Church in the Hollow" – this is one of the ruins of the Seven Churches monastery near Onaght.

Teampall Asurnai

Situated west of Kilronan and perhaps dedicated to the female saint Soarney.

Teampall Bheanáin

"St. Benan's Church", another remaining building of St. Enda's monastery.

Teampall Breacháin

"St. Brecan's Church". This is the largest ruin on the site of the Seven Churches monastery. St. Brecan, one of St. Enda's disciples founded this monastery. He is very highly honoured by the people of Aran.

Teampall na Ceathrar Álainn

"The Church of the Four Beautiful Ones". The 'beautiful ones' were said to be four saints called Fursey, Brendan of Birr, Conall and Berchan. It is located near the village of Cowrugh.

Teampall Chiaráin

"St. Kieran's Church" is situated near Mainistir, a village west of Kilronan. St. Kieran is said to be the same saint who founded the great monastery at Clonmacnoise on the River Shannon in AD 545.

Teampall MacDuach

This church is dedicated to St. Colman, patron saint of sailors. It is situated near Kilmurvey.

Teampall na Naomh

"The Church of the Saints" near Kilmurvey.

An Trá Mór

"The Big Strand", a large sandy beach on the south-east end of the island.

An Turloch Mór

A turloch (an impermanent lake) located between Killeany and Kilronan.

INISHMAAN / INIS MEÁIN (The Middle Island)

Dún Conor / Dún Chonchúir

"Conor's Fort". It is not known who Conor was. Dun Conor is a magnificent ring-fort on a hill overlooking Inishmaan.

Dún Moher

Also called Dún Fhearbhaigh (Farvey's Fort).

Kilcanaragh / Cill Cheannach

"St. Kenanagh's Church". Some say that Kenanagh is another name for St. Gregory. Gregory's Sound between Inishmore and Inishmaan is said to be named after him.

Teampall na Seacht Mac Ri

"The Church of the Seven Princes". It is not known to whom this church is dedicated.

INISHEER / INIS ÓIRR (The Eastern Island)

Cill na Seacht n'Iníon

"The Church of the Seven Daughters". It is not known who the daughters in question were.

Dún Formna

"The Fort of the Ridge". This is the only remaining fort on Inisheer. Within its walls stand the ruins of O'Brien Castle.

Teampall Chaomháin

"St. Cavan's Church" − according to legend, St. Cavan was the brother of St. Kevin of Glendalough, Co. Wicklow. The islanders pray to St. Cavan in times of illness.

Teampall Ghobnait

"St. Gobnet's Church". St. Gobnet was one of Ireland's best loved women saints. and is said to have spent some time on Inisheer. She is the patron saint of beekeepers, and is still honoured on the islands, even though nobody keeps bees there. She and St. Soarney on Inishmore are the only women saints associated with Aran.

field and shore

contents

Readers Note
The text from pages 84 to 146
of Field and Shore, although
written in the present tense, is
set around 1900.

the land
of aran

HE ARAN ISLANDS AND the Burren district
of North Clare are perhaps the most barren
parts of Ireland. Cromwell is reputed to have
said that one could not "find a tree to hang a
man, water to drown him nor earth to bury
him" in these areas. Yet, one who had a bird's
eye view of the Aran Islands could clearly see the
outline of ancient fields especially around the great
stone forts which are scattered over the islands.

We can only guess that, at some time in the distant past, the
land was much better than it has been in recent centuries. The
islands may even have been covered by forests or leafy deciduous
trees. It seems likely that the clearing of the trees allowed heavy
rainfall and strong winds to wash the soil off the rocky limestone surface. Man may have helped to destroy the fertility of the
soil by over-use and bad management. Whatever the reason, the
surface of the Aran islands, now, is a series of bare limestone
terraces. To grow their crops the islanders must make their fields
on the bare rocks.

An Aran poet, Tomás Ó Díreáin, describes the struggle of the
island farmer to make his barren land fertile.

The Aran Landscape. Bare limestone pavements, criss-crossed by fissures step up gently to a hilltop fort.

AN tÁRANNACH

Féach é ina sheasamh ar an leic,
Atá liath agus lom,
Ag guí chun Dia
Le neart agus stuaim
Go gcuirfidh sé toradh
(Le anró agus pian)
Ar an áit atá lom
Leis na mílte bliain.

Le allas a bhaithis,
Le fuil a chroí,
Déanfaidh sé talamh
As na scalpachaí.

Tomás Ó Direáin

These maps show how one townland near Kilronan has had more and more of its open rough pasture improved to make new fields.

 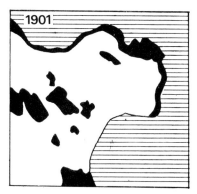

Improved Land
Rough Pasture

MAKING FIELDS

An area of flat rock which is in a suitable location is chosen. The surface is evened by knocking off any outcrops of rock, but it must not be completely smooth or the soil which is to be spread on it will not be able to grip and will be blown away.

Large cracks are filled up with pieces of rock to prevent the soil from trickling down through them. The larger stones, which were removed from the surface are used to build a wall around the 'field'. This wall will give shelter to the crops growing in the field as well as keeping out any wandering cattle or sheep.

The surface which has been prepared is then covered with layers of sand and seaweed carted up from the beach. Finally a layer of precious soil is laid on top. This soil has been gathered from the crevices between the rocks and from the more fertile parts of the island.

The writer J. M. Synge visited the Aran Islands each summer from 1898 – 1902. Here he writes about the making of a field.

"The other day the men of this house made a new field. There was a slight bank of earth under the wall of the yard and another in the corner of the cabbage garden. The old man and his eldest son dug out the clay, with the care of men working in a gold-mine, and Michael packed it in panniers – there are no wheeled vehicles on this island – for transport to a flat rock in a sheltered corner of the holding, where it was mixed with sand and seaweed and spread out in a layer upon the stone. Most of the potato growing of the island is carried on in fields of this sort – for which the people pay a considerable rent – and if the season is at all dry, their hope of a fair crop is nearly always disappointed.

It is now nine days since rain has fallen, and the people are filled with anxiety, although the sun has not yet been hot enough to do harm."

In some parts of the islands the area used for growing crops is gradually increasing as new fields are added each year. A field may be sown with potatoes as its first crop, then spend a year under a crop of rye and finally be allowed to lie fallow, or rest, for a year or two. This system is called a crop rotation – each crop follows the previous one in a set order and it is a valuable means of preserving the fertility of the soil.

Tiny stone walled fields on Inisheer. There are no gateways and a farmer will knock down and rebuild sections of a wall to allow his cows to enter and leave a pasture.

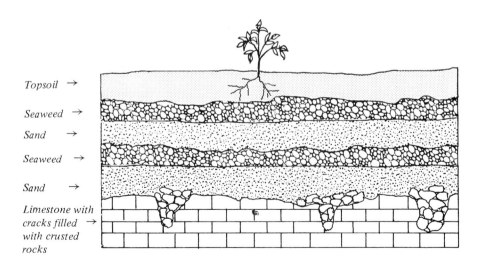

Topsoil →

Seaweed →

Sand →

Seaweed →

Sand →

Limestone with cracks filled → with crusted rocks

LAND OWNERSHIP

Each family on Aran owns its farm. This was not always so as the islanders were, until this century, tenant farmers who had to pay rent to a landlord for their small holdings. In the 1870's a series of poor harvests, especially of potatoes and oats, meant that the tenants were short of food and were unable to pay their rent to the landlords. Evictions took place in Mayo and Galway and other parts of the country and the tenants were compelled to unite to fight for their rights. In 1879 they formed the Land League to campaign for "The Three F's" —

> "Fair Rent
> Fixity of Tenure
> Freedom of Sale"

They were granted these demands by the British Parliament in Gladstone's Land Acts of 1881 and 1882. Under these acts a tenant and his family could remain on their farm even if the rent was in arrears and they also had the right to sell their interest in the farm to any other person. But the members of the Land League had tasted victory and had acquired a new aim. They now wished to get rid of landlords altogether and make each man the sole owner of his farm. The Government of the United Kingdom was forced to accept this proposal and made money available at low interest rates to the tenants so that they could buy out their holdings. The landlords were only too happy to agree and to cut their losses. By 1910, four million hectares of Irish land had changed hands under these purchase schemes. But the process of reform was slow in some areas. It was not until 1922 that the landlords, the Digby-St. Lawrence family, sold their interests in the islands and the Aran farmers became the owners of their land. Each pays a small annuity as repayment on the Land Act loan he received.

FARM AND FAMILY

The father in each family is the one who makes all the important decisions regarding the farm. His sons work beside him and learn the skills of farming from him. When he grows old he hands over the farm to one of his sons, usually the eldest, when the young man is ready for marriage. The father and mother allow the young couple to take over the running of both the farm and the house and they 'retire' from control. This arrangement often works out very well and all concerned are happy. Sometimes, though, an old man may be slow to give up control of his farm and may hang on to it until both he and his sons are quite old.

The sons often feel bitter in such a situation because, without the farm they do not have the independence and security to get married. Island men usually do not marry until they are quite old; in many cases the man is forty years of age before he has the independence to enable him to marry. Sadly, some men wait too long for a parent to hand over the land or to die, and find that they are too old to marry when they eventually receive their inheritance. Not all young people are prepared to wait; some prefer to emigrate and give up their claim to the farm completely.

Parents are not always at fault, of course. The young couple may become too bossy or may not pay enough regard to the knowledge, experience and age of the old couple. Friction between the old mother and the young wife is regarded by the islanders as a great misfortune. They know that it can make for a very unhappy household.

In Aran, land is fairly evenly divided among the farmers, each holding consisting of 7 to 8 hectares. Most farmers also own a portion of sea-shore where they can gather seaweed for fertilizer. Each person has some good fields suitable for growing his potatoes and grazing his cattle. In addition he has some rough grazing for sheep and some of the almost useless bare stone flagging. This means, of course, that a man's fields may be widely scattered. Such a farm is described as fragmented.

FIELD PATTERNS

Distinctive field patterns are found in different parts of Ireland and they are an important clue to the type of farming carried on locally. In the fertile grazing lands of Meath, farms are large and the density of population is low. Fields are also large in order to facilitate the grazing of cattle. But in West Galway and the Aran Islands the land is poor and the farms are very small. The irregular pattern of tiny stone walled fields reflects this.

STONE WALLS

Each little field is surrounded by a stone wall. The walls are quite high, forming a maze for the stranger who can find himself going round in circles. The walls are a convenient place where the

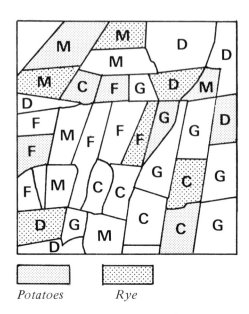

This diagram shows a 28 hectare section of one of the islands. There are forty fields in all owned by five different farmers. The owner of each field is identified by the initial letter of his name on the map.

Potatoes   Rye

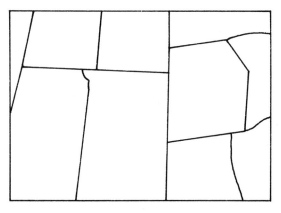

Left shows a field pattern in Co. Meath, where the fields are large compared to the small fields of Aran

½ KM

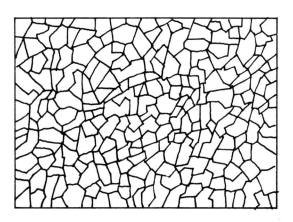

farmer can put the rocks and boulders which he clears from his land. They also protect the precious soil and crops in each field from the strong Atlantic winds. The walls are modern examples of the dry stone masonry found in the ancient forts. No mortar or cement is used in their building. The stones are carefully selected and positioned so that the wind may pass freely through the gaps between them. In this way the wall can withstand the fierce force of the south westerly gales. Wind passing through the walls often makes an eerie whistling sound over the islands.

GATES

Metal and timber must be imported from the mainland and so are in short supply on the islands. Therefore 'gates' in the walls are also made of rocks. When a wall is being built, an entrance gap, several feet wide, is left open. When the wall is completed the gap is filled with rounded stones. Each time a farmer wishes to drive his cattle into the field he knocks down this 'gate'. The rounded stones tumble down quite easily and can be rebuilt without much trouble, afterwards.

CROPS

The little fields produce potatoes and rye, mainly for use on the islands. Vegetables such as cabbage, onions and lettuce are sometimes grown in little plots of land around the houses. Here and there, willows, for basket making, are grown in small enclosures.

Potatoes are the most common crop in Aran, and as in the rest of the country, they are a staple in the diet of the people. The potato is easily grown and thrives in a damp climate. It has an extremely high yield and even poor land will produce up to 15 tonnes per hectare. This makes it an attractive crop for the small farmer who has a limited amount of land available for tillage. In addition, the potato has a very high food value and, combined with milk, bread, fish and meat, makes for a nourishing, well-balanced diet. In large, fertile fields potatoes are sown with the aid of a horse-drawn plough in long, single rows. But in the small, stony fields of Aran the potatoes must be sown by manual labour. Using only a spade the farmer plants his potatoes in wide ridges known as lazybeds. First of all, narrow trenches, about 50 centimetres in width, are dug with a spade. The trenches are spaced over 1 metre intervals and layers of seaweed are spread on the ground between each pair. Sods from the trench are turned over, grassy side down, on top of the seaweed, to build up a 'ridge'. The rotting of the grass and seaweed will provide vital nutrients to feed the growing crop. More seaweed and, finally, a layer of soil are added. The potato seeds are planted in this top layer, in rows of three or four.

Two months after planting, more soil is dug from the trenches and added to the ridge to protect and strengthen the young plants. The potato patch may be weeded several times and when the potato stalks have attained their full height they will be sprayed with a mixture of bluestone and water to prevent blight.

The potato seed is selected in mid January. Potatoes retained from the previous crop are cut into sections, each of which must have an 'eye'. The fields are prepared and planting or 'seeding' takes place in March and early April. It is very important for the islanders to sow potatoes on time. "A person who is lazy about planting, is lazy about everything" they say. A farmer who is late with his 'seeding' is contemptuously referred to as a "Cuckoo farmer" because he is still seeding when the first call of the cuckoo is heard in May.

Potatoes are harvested from the end of July onwards. They are sorted in the fields into seed potatoes, cattle feed, and high quality potatoes for human consumption. They are stored in outhouses or in pits until needed. A pit is a shallow trench in which the potatoes are placed. They are covered over with hay or straw and finally with a layer of earth or sods. The potatoes will then be safe from both frost and field animals. Only in a very wet year does the crop yield a surplus beyond the family's immediate needs. This surplus, when it occurs, is sold on the mainland.

Rye is the only grain crop grown on the islands. It thrives in a damp, cool climate and grows well even on soils which are poor and thin. The tough rye straw is used for thatching the island houses and is also used as a bedding and a feeding stuff for cattle. The grain yield is sufficient only to provide seed for next year's planting.

The rye crop is sown in autumn, after the potatoes have been lifted. Most farmers rotate their potato and rye crops in order to allow the soil to renew the different nutrients which each crop drains from it. Harvesting takes place in June.

Rye, which is to be used for thatching, is pulled rather than cut. It is tied in bundles and propped against a wall to dry in the

Above – *The method of making lazybeds for growing potatoes. The soil is cut and turned back on itself.*
Below – *Lazybeds in a potato garden in Inisheer in early Summer. In the background is the 15th century O'Brien Castle and the outline of Dun Formna which surrounds it.*

summer sun. The islanders prefer to pull the rye because the roots, which remain attached to the straw, prevent the bundles from slipping when they are laid on a roof for use by the thatcher.

The dry bundles of rye are threshed to separate the grain from the stalks. Two large stones are stood on end, leaning against each other. The bundles, or sheaves, are beaten individually, against the stones until the grain falls away. This is known as *flailing.* The seed is still wrapped in a dry skin called chaff. It is dropped, a handful at a time onto a dry, flat rock surface, while the wind blows the chaff away. This is known as *winnowing.* The grain is used as seed for the next year's crop.

If the rye is to be used as an animal feed it is cut, using a scythe, while it is still 'green' and has not, as yet, ripened fully. The farmer rakes it into parallel rows for drying, turning it every now and then. When dry, it is carefully stacked in ricks which are tied down with strong grass ropes, *súgáns,* to prevent them blowing away.

The harvesting of the crops is the most vital activity in the yearly cycle of farmwork. It is a time of worry and anxiety for the farmer because bad weather can delay the harvest or prevent the rye from drying properly, making it useless for its intended purpose.

When all the crops have been harvested, great celebrations take place. The spade is ceremoniously placed in the fire for a few moments, to show that it is no longer needed. The helpers and neighbours who have assisted in the harvest are invited to a *féil searra* – a céilí to mark the successful end to a year's work on the land.

FARM ANIMALS

The visitor to Aran is frequently impressed by the fact that each farmer keeps one or more cows, even though the farms are tiny, the land poor and grass extremely scarce. Cattle are very highly valued on the islands. The size of a farm is seldom described in acres. The islanders prefer to say "He has the grass of two cows."

Cattle are grazed on scattered patches of grassland which have been cordoned off for the purpose. They are left in the fields all year round, despite the bad weather. During a severe winter, when there is not enough grass to graze on, the farmer will carry bundles of rye to the fields for his cows. When nothing else is available, he may even feed them on a mixture of bran and

Above– Goats are kept by many families. They seek out patches of grass and are an important part of the economy, providing milk and hides.

Left – Cows are seldom housed in a byre on Aran, but are left in the fields both Summer and Winter. A common sight is that of women or young men coming or going from distant fields with a milk-can.

potatoes. Cattle must be very sturdy to survive in the harsh environment of the islands. The young calf is allowed to suckle its mother's milk for a much longer period than is common on the mainland. Though this means less milk for themselves, the islanders feel that it is worthwhile in order to rear a strong fat calf.

One or more dairy cows supply the milk requirements of each household. The cows are milked in the fields, which are often at a considerable distance from the farmhouse. Each milch cow yields little more than 1800 litres per annum due to the harsh conditions and poor grass. Whereas, in a fertile area like the Golden Vale a cow may yield twice this quantity. Some of this milk is fed to calves; some of it is churned at home to make butter; most of it is consumed in liquid form.

Cattle are sold at regular fairs held on all three islands. Sales are highest in the early summer and at the great Michaelmas fairs held on the 28th September. The farmers sell off their surplus stock at this time as grass will probably be scarce during the winter. The buyers, or cattle jobbers as they are called, come from Galway, and they take the animals to the mainland for fattening on good grassland before exporting them to England.

Horses are also sold at these fairs and pigs may be disposed of at regular intervals or slaughtered and salted down for home consumption.

Sheep and goats are also kept by many farmers on the islands. These animals are well suited to Aran. They are allowed to roam freely over the rough pastures and rocky hills seeking out grass in the crevices between the slabs of limestone. Sheep supply meat and, more importantly wool. The goats provide milk and hides. Some farmers also keep pigs which are housed in enclosures in the farmyard and are fed on boiled potatoes, domestic scraps and skimmed milk left over after buttermaking.

The donkey is the favourite beast of burden on the islands. He is sure footed and nimble on the rocky surface and he requires neither farm cart nor roadway. The farmer straps two wicker baskets, or panniers, across the donkey's back, and in these he transports seaweed from the shore and potatoes and rye from the fields. He may ride on the donkey when travelling to his outlying fields or hitch a small cart to the animal when collecting supplies from pier head or beach, after delivery by the steamer. Some horses and ponies are also kept but the versatile donkey is a more useful beast in such conditions.

Occasionally an islander may go to Galway to buy farm animals — a cow, a donkey, or perhaps a horse. Getting an animal home to Inisheer or Inishmaan may pose a problem as the steamer cannot come to land in either of these islands. The animals are generally hoisted by rope from the steamer's deck and gently lowered into the water behind a waiting curragh. Two men in the stern of the curragh hold the animal with a halter allowing it to swim ashore behind the boat. Smaller animals, such as pigs and sheep, have their legs tied together and they are bundled into the curragh along with the rest of the cargo.

BELIEFS AND CUSTOMS

All over Ireland, particularly in areas where land is of poor quality, such as Aran, farmers practice age-old customs which are believed to be of benefit in preserving the fertility of the land.

Bad luck is said to follow if a farmer misses out a line when planting a ridge of potatoes. A fistful of salt may be sprinkled on a field to preserve the fertility of the soil.

If a funeral passes through a farm it brings bad luck to the land but a goat, kept with a herd of cows, may bring good luck.

The first stream of milk from a newly calved cow is allowed to fall to the ground "for those who might need it".

Many customs and beliefs concerning the land are related to particular times of the year. The feast of the Holy Innocents, *Lá na Leanbh,* falls on December 28th and is also known as The Cross Day, *Lá Crosta na Bliana.* If, for instance, this feast happens to occur on a Monday, then every Monday throughout that year will be a 'Cross day'. It is regarded as unlucky to get married or to dig a grave on such a day and bad luck may follow if the planting or the harvesting of crops is begun on 'Cross day'.

Work which involves any actions of turning or twisting including any form of digging, is never performed on St. Brigid's Day — *Bionn Lá Le Bríde ina shaoire ar chasaibh,* St. Brigid's Day is free from twisting, the people say. A similar prohibition exists concerning November 11th, St. Martin's Day.

On Good Friday, adults and weaned children never drink milk but it is regarded as lucky to plant some seed potatoes on that day. The Feast of St. John on 24th June corresponds to the ancient festival of Midsummer. On St. John's Eve bonfires are lit in every village and the farmers throw a blazing bush into the potato gardens and rye fields to bring luck.

Left – The 'steamer' taking a cow on board at Kilronan for transport to the mainland.

Below – The Cruel Sea – exerting a mighty force on the Atlantic coastlines of all three islands. The bedding planes of limestones and shale can be identified in the sheer face of the cliffs which rise in the background.

the sea

OR FIVE HUNDRED KILOMETRES the sea floor slopes gently westwards from the Irish coast before plunging abruptly to the ocean depths. This shallow submarine area is known as the Continental Shelf. The waters on the Continental Shelf are penetrated, almost to the very bottom, by the sun's rays. They are warmed by the current of the North Atlantic Drift, flowing across the ocean from the Gulf of Mexico. Hundreds of rivers and streams bring billions of tiny animals down to this sea. It is a rich feeding ground, teeming with many species of fish.

Most farmers on Aran are fishermen too. The sea has provided food for the islanders over the centuries. It has allowed them to supplement the meagre living which they wring from their rocky fields. It has protected them in times of invasion, and in hungry famine years it has given them the food which saved them from starvation. But the sea is also cruel. It has isolated the islanders, battering them with violent storms and cutting them off, over long periods, from human contact and medical aid. Time and again it has claimed the lives of the island men.

The islanders respect the sea, knowing the dangers of its ever changing moods. They know and understand the workings of wind and weather, tide and wave. They handle their boats with care and skill.

Very few of the islanders can swim. They like to say that if you cannot swim, you'll be more careful on the sea, and that for the non-swimmer, death by drowning will be quicker and without a struggle.

In this passage from Synge's *Riders to the Sea* Old Maurya is lamenting for the children she has lost to the sea and expressing her conviction that her youngest son Bartley will now also be drowned. Her daughter Nora tries to console her.

NORA: Didn't the young priest say the Almighty God won't leave her destitute with no son living?

MAURYA (*in a low voice, but clearly*): It's little the like of him knows of the sea.... Bartley will be lost by now, and let you call in Eamon and make me a good coffin out of the white boards, for I won't live after them. I've had a husband, and a husband's father, and six sons in this house — six fine men, though it was a hard birth I had with every one of them and they coming to the world — and some of them were found and some of them were not found, but they're gone now the lot of them... There were Stephen and Shawn were lost in the great wind, and found after in the Bay of Gregory of the Golden Mouth, and carried up the two of them on one plank, and in by that door.

CATHLEEN (*in a whisper*): There's someone after crying out by the seashore.

MAURYA (*continues without hearing anything*): There was Sheamus and his father, and his own father again, were lost in a dark night, and not a stick or sign was seen of them when the sun went up. There was Patch after was drowned out of a curragh that turned over. I was sitting here with Bartley, and he a baby lying on my two knees, and I seen two women, and three women, and four women coming in, and they crossing themselves and not saying a word. I looked out then, and there were men coming after them, and they holding a thing in the half of a red sail, and water dripping out of it — it was a dry day, Nora — and leaving a track to the door.

THE CLEGGAN DISASTER

In 1927, twenty-five fishermen from the Cleggan area of Co. Galway were drowned in a storm while fishing. This excerpt is from Richard Murphy's long poem *The Cleggan Disaster.*

Whose is that hulk on the shingle
The boatwright's son repairs
Though she has not been fishing
For thirty-four years
Since she rode the disaster?
The oars were turned into rafters
For a roof stripped by a gale.
Moss has grown on her keel.

Where are the red-haired women
Chattering along the piers
Who gutted millions of mackerel
And baited the spillet hooks
With mussels and lug-worms?
All the hurtful hours
Thinking the boats were coming
They hold against those years.

Where are the barefoot children
With brown toes in the ashes
Who went to the well for water,
Picked winkles on the beach
And gathered sea-rods in winter?
The lime is green on the stone
Which they once kept white-washed.
In summer nettles return.

Where are the dances in houses
With porter and cakes in the room,
The reddled faces of fiddlers
Sawing out jigs and reels,
The flickering eyes of neighbours?
The thatch which was neatly bordered
By a fringe of sea-stones
Has now caved in.

Why does she stand at the curtains
Combing her seal-grey hair
And uttering bitter opinions
On land-work and sea-fear,
Drownings and famines?
When will her son say,
"Forget about the disaster,
We're mounting nets today!"

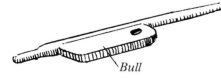

Curragh Oar

Scale c. 1/24

Bull

THE SEA

I am patient, repetitive, multi-voiced,
Yet few hear me
And fewer still trouble to understand

Why, for example, I caress
And hammer the land.
I do not brag of my depths

Or my currents, I do not
Boast of my moods or my colours
Or my breath in your thought.

In time I surrender my drowned,
My appetite speaks for itself,
I could swallow all you have found

And open for more,
My green tongues licking the shores
Of the world

Like starved beasts reaching for men
Who will not understand
When I rage and roar

When I bellow and threaten
I am obeying a law
Observing a discipline.

This is the rhythm
I live.
This is the reason I move

In hunger and skill
To give you the pick of my creatures.
This is why I am willing to kill,

Chill every created nerve.
You have made me a savage master
Because I know how to serve.

Brendan Kennelly

BOATS

The curragh is an open canoe which is ideally suited to conditions in the Aran Islands. She can ride successfully in almost any sea and weather conditions; she slips rapidly over the surface of calm water but she can just as easily cope with the mountainous white crested waves of a stormy sea. The curragh needs neither pier nor harbour as she can be run ashore on any smooth patch of sand or gravel. Three men can hoist an upturned curragh onto their shoulders without undue strain and lay her on a stone 'cradle' above high tide mark until she will be needed again. A curragh being transported in this way looks, from above, like a gigantic six-legged beetle.

The islanders are dependent on the curragh for the transporting of their everyday needs. People, animals and goods are all carted in the curragh and she is invaluable in those islands which do not have a harbour where steamer or hooker can safely land.

The ancient curraghs were made from the skins of animals, particularly cowhides, but more recently the materials needed have been brought in from the mainland. For the Aran Islands curragh a light wooden frame is first constructed using (in the three-man model) thirty ribs spaced 14 centimetres apart. The ribs are sawn laths, the dimensions of which are 4 cm. by 1.5 cm. The gunwhales are fashioned from wood also and are about 7 cm. wide by 5 cms. deep. Heavy canvas is then stretched over this frame and securely fastened. Finally, the boat receives several coats of tar to make her waterproof. When complete the three-man Aran curragh is 6 metres long and a four-man boat may measure up to 8 metres. The beam, or breadth of the boat at the centre, varies from about 8 metres and its depth is about 1 metre. If a curragh is handled with care and promptly repaired it should give at least eight years of service. A hole in the canvas of the boat is easily repaired by its owner. The tar around the hole is melted. A piece of canvas is then placed over it and then tarred over several times until it is almost invisible. Although the Aran curragh is now constructed from modern materials the primitive design is still retained. It has been tried and proved over the centuries and still gives good service to the islanders.

ROWING A CURRAGH

A curragh has no keel, and so depends on the skill of her oarsmen and on ballast for her grip on the water. Ballast is extra weight carried in a boat to make her 'sit' safely in the water and in Aran it takes the form of carefully chosen round boulders.

The curragh is rowed with long, narrow, bladeless oars. Each oarsman rows with two of these oars, the hole in the "Bull" of the oar sitting over a wooden tholepin or peg which stands vertically on the gunwhale of the boat. This allows the oar to pivot back and forth but it cannot be swept away, if, for any reason, the oarsman should let loose his grip. Rowing and steering a curragh require great skill. The oarsman must also be a good judge of the opportune moment for launching and beaching the boat. A mistake could result in the boat being smashed or swamped and in her crew being lost.

Sometimes a simple sail is rigged in a curragh and an oar is extended over the stern to act as a steer.

John Millington Synge described the launching of a curragh:

'In bad weather, four men will often stand for nearly an hour at the top of the slip with a curragh in their hands, watching a point of rock towards the south where they can see the strength of the waves that are coming in.

The instant a break is seen, they swoop down to the surf, launch their curragh, and pull out to sea with incredible speed. Coming to land is attended with the same difficulty, and, if the moment is badly chosen, they are likely to be washed sideways and swamped among the rocks.'

But bringing a curragh to land could be even more dangerous as he soon discovered.

'Late this evening, I saw a three-oared curragh with two old women in her besides the rowers, landing at the slip through a heavy roll. They were coming from Inisheer, and they rowed up quickly enough till they were within a few yards of the surf-line, where they spun round and waited with the prow towards the sea, while wave after wave passed underneath them and broke on the remains of the slip. Five minutes passed; ten minutes; and still they waited with the oars just paddling in the water, and their heads turned over their shoulders.

I was beginning to think they would have to give up and row

The Aran Island Curragh

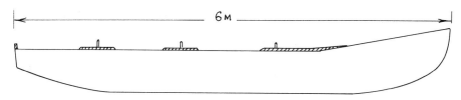

6 M

ELEVATION

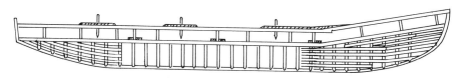

A.Monnelly　　　ELEVATION　(without canvas, laths not completed)

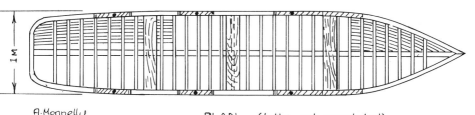

1 M

A.Monnelly　　　PLAN　(laths not completed)

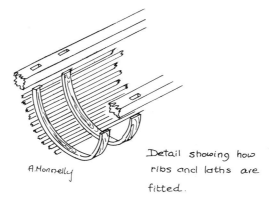

A.Monnelly

Detail showing how ribs and laths are fitted.

Hookers at Kilronan pier around 1890. Their curved side planks and single stout mast are distinctive. On the left is a large two masted sailing trawler of the kind used in Aran waters by Arklow fishermen. A steamer has moored in the bay as it cannot approach the pier at low tide. Row boats are busy ferrying visitors to and from the ship.

round to the lee side of the island, when the curragh seemed suddenly to turn into a living thing. The prow was again towards the slip, leaping and hurling itself through the spray. Before it touched, the man in the bow wheeled round, two white legs came out over the prow like the flash of a sword, and before the next wave arrived he had dragged the curragh out of danger.

This sudden and united action in men without discipline shows well the education that the waves have given them. When the curragh was in safety the two old women were carried up through the surf and slippery seaweed on the backs of their sons.

In this broken weather a curragh cannot go out without danger, yet accidents are rare and seem to be nearly always caused by drink. Since I was here last year four men have been drowned on their way home from the large island. First a curragh belonging to the south island which put off with two men in her heavy with drink, came to shore here the next evening dry and uninjured, with the sail half set and no one in her.

More recently a curragh from this island with three men, who were the worse for drink was upset on its way home. The steamer was not far off, and saved two of the men, but could not reach the third."

THE GALWAY HOOKER

A large wooden hulled boat, the Galway Bay Hooker, sometimes called the Connemara Hooker, is used by the mainlanders for fishing, shark hunting and carting turf to the islands. They are single masted sailing boats which are easily recognisable by their dark brown sails and high, tarred hull.

THE SEA

Look you out
northeastwards
Over mighty ocean,
Teeming with sea-life;
Home of seals,
Sporting, splendid,
Its tide has reached
fullness.

(Medieval Irish Lyric)

A group of Kilronan fishermen dressed in the traditional bawneens and pampooties. A two-masted sailing trawler is berthed at the pier. In the bay an ice hulk is anchored to supply ice for keeping trawl fish fresh until it can be shipped to market in Galway. Straw Island and its lighthouse are in the background.

FISHING

Over thirty varieties of fish are found in the waters around the Aran Islands and the islanders fish for many of these at various times of the year. The fishermen use different types of gear to land the particular species.

DRIFT NETS

Drift nets are nets which float in an upright position near the surface creating a 'wall' into which mackerel and herring blindly swim. 'Drifting' is carried on at night when the nets are invisible to the fish and the shoals rise nearer to the surface. The islanders use curraghs for this work but, since 1892, Aranmen have fished on large wooden, sailing drifters which visit Galway Bay for the rich spring and autumn mackerel fishery. These boats, from the east coast of Ireland, land large catches which are salted down for export to America. This large scale 'curing' operation provides valuable seasonal employment for women.

LONG LINES

Long lines are used to catch those fish which live on, or near, the sea bed and which include 'round' fish like cod, ling and pollock, and 'flat' fish like plaice, sole and turbot. The long lines, as the name suggests are lines of about 200–300 metres in length which have 100 or more hooks attached. The hooks are baited with slugs or salt fish and the long line is anchored in a suitable location and left out overnight. Two buoys, one at either end, mark the place where the line has been set.

POTS

Lines of pots are used to catch shellfish such as lobster and crayfish. The pots for catching lobster are made from willow, and those for crayfish are made from thin laths. They are weighted with stones and have baits fixed inside an opening. Several pots are attached at intervals to a rope and they are lowered to the sea bed. A buoy or float at either end marks the spot.

The pots may be hauled and rebaited several times in the course

The most important species of fish found in Aran waters are:

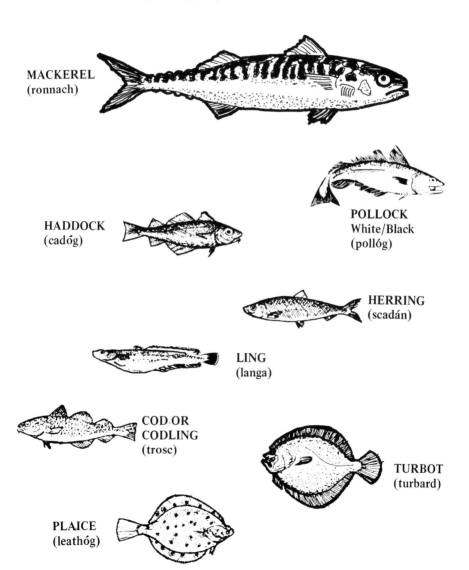

MACKEREL
(ronnach)

POLLOCK
White/Black
(pollóg)

HADDOCK
(cadóg)

HERRING
(scadán)

LING
(langa)

COD OR
CODLING
(trosc)

TURBOT
(turbard)

PLAICE
(leathóg)

of the day. The lobsters which have crawled in through the narrow basket shaped entrance are trapped and cannot climb out again. They are stored in a floating crate made of wood, through which the sea freely passes and they are marketed weekly or when a sufficient quantity has been gathered. This type of fishing can only be conducted in the very calmest summer weather as it involves working close to cliffs and submerged reefs. The catch is valuable and a good season can boost the finances of island families but the risks involved are considerable.

HAND LINES

Hand lines are used occasionally to catch mackerel, pollock and bass. They may be worked from a curragh but fishing from the cliff tops is quite common. The islander squats at the very edge of a sheer drop, up to one hundred metres above the ocean surface, and casts and hauls his line from this dangerous position.

'CURING' FISH

Mackerel, herring, cod, pollock and ling which are not sold immediately must be 'cured' for winter use. The cleaned and gutted fish may be packed into a barrel containing a pickle made of coarse salt and fresh water. Mackerel and herring are usually cured in this way. Cod and ling may be pickled lightly in a barrel for a short period, then hung on the rafters or spread on a flat stone to dry. When 'cured' the fish will keep for a considerable time and will retain their food value and their flavour.

SHARKS

In the past sharks were more often found in the waters around Aran. They were hunted and killed with harpoons by the islanders who would cut out the liver and discard the body of the shark. The liver of a single shark could, when boiled, produce up to 900 litres of oil which is used for domestic lighting.

BELIEFS AND CUSTOMS

Fishing is an occupation which offers varying rewards. In a sense the fisherman takes his life in his hands each time he launches a curragh. Safety at sea and a good catch can never be guaranteed. Therefore the fisherman takes precautions to avoid damaging his luck, as he sees it.

If the fisherman, on the way to the shore, meets a red-haired or barefoot woman, it is regarded as a bad omen for the day's work. Meeting a hare, a rabbit, a priest or a fox is also regarded as being unlucky and, while at sea, the fishermen avoid mentioning a priest, or a pig or a weasel. Three men of the same name must not fish together nor should anybody smoke while at his work. When at home, a fisherman is careful not to throw a fish bone in the fire.

Boats never put to sea on a Saturday night nor do they fish on St. Martin's Day, the 11th of November, or the eve of Michaelmas which falls on the 28th September. Nets are lowered into the water in the name of God, Mary and St. Peter and the rosary is often recited at midnight while the men wait to haul.

A fleet of iron masted trawlers and single masted hookers at Kilronan around 1890.

the shore

N THE HARSH ISLAND ENVIRONMENT every resource which nature offers must be utilised if a man is to be successful in his struggle to feed and clothe his family. The shore, as well as the land and the ocean offers plentiful resources. Both sand and seaweed play an important role in the economy of the islands.

FERTILISER

The only fertilisers available to the Aran farmer who wishes to improve his stony fields are sand and seaweed. The sand found on the Aran beaches has been created by the erosion of limestone rock. It is highly calcareous and is of benefit in growing potatoes. Certain kinds of seaweed can serve the same function and are hauled to the fields at seeding time, using a donkey and panniers.

KELP

Kelp is an iodine-rich substance which is produced by burning red seaweed. The islanders sell this to factories on the mainland where it is used in the making of chemicals and drugs. The red weed grows under water and is best gathered after the autumn and winter storms. Often the islanders must wade thigh deep in the icy water to cut the seaweed from submerged rocks so the work must be done on a calm day when tides are low. Knives and sickles attached to long handles are used for cutting the weed from the deeper water. This deep-water weed is prized, as it is entirely free of sand.

Sea-rods, which are the stalks of seaweeds, being stacked. They are exported for chemical processing. One of the main extracts is iodine.

The wet seaweed is carried up from the shore in panniers by donkey. It is hard, heavy work, as it takes more than 25 tonnes of weed to make one tonne of kelp and the work must be completed quickly while tides are favourable. If a family does not own a donkey they must carry the weed in baskets on their backs. Because the men are busy cutting the weed, women sometimes do this work wearing an animal hide on their back to protect their clothing.

When gathered, the weed is laid out to dry on walls and rocks and then piled up in ricks, not unlike haycocks, where it is left until early June. June is the usual time for burning the kelp. A kelp kiln, a low, rectangular stone trough, capable of holding about two tonnes of weed, is constructed for burning the dry seaweed. Firing must be done properly as the kelp may be ruined if not given enough time to 'run' or if fired for too long. As the weed begins to melt it is stirred with long iron rakes until it turns into a molten mass. When the firing is complete the kelp is left to cool in the kiln. After a few days the substance is as hard as limestone and has to be broken up with a sledge hammer before it is transported in curraghs to Kilronan. There it is tested for quality and the kelp-burner is paid. Later, the steamer will take it to the mainland.

Thomas O'Flaherty, an islander, writes about a conversation he had with one of his neighbours, Old Michael, when the old man was burning his kelp. The islanders have discovered that if they do not stir the kelp as it burns, it will emerge as a powder, equally rich in iodine, but much easier to manage and transport as it can be packed into bags.

' "And doesn't the kelp run at all now and don't you have to break it up with a sledge?"

"Damn the run,....: They say it's better to have her in small stones or in powder. We put her all in bags now. In your time there was no respect at all for the kelp that was in the bags. Everything is different now. We don't work as hard as we used to and though there is no money we live better than we ever did. We are eating meat now my boy!"

"How many tons are you going to have, Michael?" I asked.

"Now .... I wouldn't like to say anything rash, but if I don't send five tons over to Kilronan I hope I may not be alive a year from to-day. That kiln is twenty feet long if she is an inch. She is three feet wide and a foot and a half in height. I'll have to burn another one. That's not bad work for a year, and we planted a lot of potatoes. Of course I have the help, God bless them. But even so it's good work and I going on my seventy-five. And only for the bad reports we had all the year about the price I'd have another ton."

"You'll have the price of the turf anyhow, Michael."

"Faith I will and enough to buy five times as much as I need. If she doesn't test six pounds a ton at least may I be stricken dead if I ever make another ton."

"That's a rash threat, Michael," I said.

"Ah sure that's only talk," he laughed. "We have to be saying something. I'd be making kelp if I never got a penny for it through force of habit. *Sé an nádúr agam é.*"

And so I walked home up the shore from Poll na Luinge with the pleasant smell of the burning seaweed in my nostrils and the soothing poteen in my blood. What a great life it was, surely, burning kelp, fishing and planting potatoes in Aran.'

WRACK

The islands are self-sufficient in many of the essentials of life. A man may build a house and a boat and feed and clothe his family from the resources available to him locally. But he cannot provide timber or fuel as there are no trees on the island. Such items must be imported from the mainland and paid for in cash. Kelp and cattle may pay for the turf but timber, for house-building and other purposes, is almost beyond the financial means of the islanders.

Driftwood, washed up on the beaches and on the rock platforms which fringe the base of the cliffs, offers a solution to this problem. Stormy weather may bring a floating harvest of planks and spars but the islanders greet the appearance of wreckage with mixed feelings. They know that their good luck must certainly mean misfortune for other human beings.

Thomas O'Flaherty describes an expedition in which he joined his father and a group of other men to gather wrack.

'It was half ebb when we got to the Port of the Fort's Mouth. Old villagers who were too shaky to risk the tall cliffs prowled among the boulders picking up a plank here and there. Out in the mouth of the little bay planks were carried back and forth by the current. Now and then a barrel rolled over. What was in the barrels? Rum, oil, grease, tar?   We would know later.

My father could hardly restrain the men from picking up stray pieces of timber. "Wait until we get to the Blind Sound," he said. "We'll gather more in one hour there than we would gather here all day."

We walked along the cliff peering at the sea. The surface of the water was unbroken as the wind had died down. Long, lazy swells rolled in from the deep, crested, and broke on the shallows. Every once in a while an exclamation would burst from one of the men:

"Look south-westerly from you, where the seagulls are! There's a whole ship load of timber there."

Suddenly I wondered what happened to the sailors who manned the wrecked vessel and I shuddered as I visualised myself going down to death in that terrible sea. Groups of men from Gort na gCapall and from Kilmurvey had picked choice spots along the cliff at and near the Blind Sound. Our advance agents had a good place. The limestone rock on the cliff's edge was smooth and would not fray the cable. The cliff was straight until within five fathoms of the bottom. There were no jutting rocks on the face of the cliff to catch the planks as they were being hauled up.

Nobody had gone down yet as there was very little of the shore at the bottom dry. Planks were piled among the rocks. Sometimes a sea would drive a plank end on against a rock and split it. Men often had their legs broken in similar situations. We were all watching the precious timber below. Hundreds of planks were suddenly left dry by a receding wave.

"Time to go down," said Bartley Pat. The cable was lashed around his body. He stood on the top of the cliff and took off his cap.

"Now, in the name of the Father, Son and Holy Ghost," he said. He turned his back to the sea, his face to the land and disappeared over the edge.

Little Jimmy was watching the descent from a vantage point and giving us directions with his hands. We lowered gradually. When Bartley had touched bottom we hauled up the rope and let the other two men down. All along the cliff men were descending, dancing in and out, steering themselves with one hand, the other holding on to the rope, striking the cliff with the sole of one foot swinging gracefully out and in until they landed at the bottom. It was a feat that called for daring and experience.

Soon we were hauling up planks and hiding them in the scalps. The coastguards would lay claim to the wrack in the name of the

The curraghs land the goods at Inishmaan.

King of England if they found it.

Furiously we worked. The men at the bottom kept sending up planks until the tide came in again. Two of them were hauled up. Then it was Bartley Pat's turn. Little Jimmy raised his hand.

We started to haul. Nobody was watching Jimmy. We were thinking about the timber.

Little Jimmy was frantically signalling us to lower. We payed out the rope slowly. "Very slowly," he signalled. We did not know what was the matter until we brought Bartley to the top.

"I thought I was as dead as a pickled herring," he chuckled. "Little Jimmy thought I gave him the signal to haul while I only wanted more rope. I only had one leg in the coil when ye hauled and I was hoisted half way up the cliff by the ankle."

"You weren't born to be hanged by the legs," my father remarked.

We put in the best part of a week gathering wrack. After the timber was safely stored away in deep clefts and caves, the coast-guards visited the village and asked if any timber was washed ashore at the Point of the Fort's Mouth. The villagers advised them that there wasn't a stick to be seen there. The coastguards thanked them for the information and returned to their quarters in Kilronan.'

the home

HE TRADITIONAL ARAN HOUSE TYPE is well suited to the windswept, stormy conditions found on the western seaboard. It is a long, low, single-storied cottage with a thatched roof. Though the size of these houses may vary considerably they all share the same basic design. They are rectangular structures with thick stone walls mortared with clay or cement. Windows and doors are set in the long side of the house rather than in the gables. The roof is steeply pitched and its weight is borne upon the walls. All have an open hearth at floor level, with a chimney protruding through the roof ridge. The walls are usually covered with whitewash which is renewed every year. There are of course other house types to be found on the islands, such as the two storied slate-roofed houses which can be seen in Kilronan and some of the larger settlements. The traditional house, however, is well adapted to climatic conditions on the island and it has the added advantage of using locally available materials. Windows are small, and are deeply set in the walls. In the past some cottages had no windows at all as rent was often calculated by the landlord on the basis of the number and size of the windows. In any case, small windows are suited to local conditions, and the combination of thick stone walls, thatched roof, and small windows with even smaller panes of glass, keeps the house warm in winter, and pleasantly cool in summer.

Doors are set in the front and back of the house. One or other almost always remains open by day, both as a means of ventilating the house and as a sign of welcome to callers. The front door may

Above – Aran houses. Thick dry stone walls make the house snug in winter and cool in summer. The roof thatch is criss-crossed with sugans or grass ropes, which are tied down as a protection against the storms of winter. The outhouse on the right is a more basic structure. It is of dry stone construction, that is, no mortar has been used in the walls, a building technique practised on Aran for several thousand years. The gable 'steps up' to the roof ridge in this type of building.

Below – Ground plans of two variations on the basic house type which are frequently found in coastal locations. One has the hearth set in the gable wall. In the other the hearth is set into the dividing wall in the centre of the house. In both cases the rooms occupy the full width of the house and open into one another.

gable hearth type

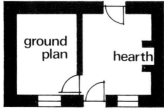

central hearth type

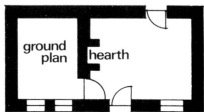

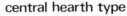

be divided in two horizontally and on windy days only the top half is opened to prevent draughts. This half-door arrangement is useful for keeping young children indoors and for preventing farm animals from entering. It also provides a comfortable arm rest for the woman of the house when she leans out and chats with her neighbours.

There are many traditional beliefs regarding the back door which are still respected. It is considered unlucky for a stranger to leave the house by the back door. When a death has occurred in the house it is customary to carry the coffin out through the back door.

BUILDING A HOUSE

Sometimes, when a young man marries he may leave the family home and build his own house with the help of friends and neighbours. The site for a house is carefully chosen, taking account of slope, shelter and distance from other dwellings. The work of building the house is carried on in a cheerful atmosphere. When completed the owner invites his helpers and neighbours to a house warming *céili* which is an occasion for general celebration.

THATCHING

When the building is finished and the roof rafters have been positioned the thatcher is called in. The thatcher is a respected craftsman who is much in demand in spring, summer and autumn. To keep the roof fully waterproofed the thatch must be repaired each year and the whole thatch must be completely renewed after seven or eight years.

The Aran houses have a gable roof which means that high gable walls rise up to the roof ridge. This arrangement is ideal for windy coastal areas. Elsewhere in Ireland traditional houses have a four sided or "hip roof" where the thatch slopes down at the sides to meet the gable at the same height as it meets the front wall.

Thatching is a reasonably cheap way of roofing a house as the materials used are available locally. It provides a warm, dry roof in winter, and, when secured properly with ropes and weights, it can withstand the fierce Atlantic gales.

It must be repaired and renewed often however, and there is always a risk that a stray spark can set the whole roof on fire.

Tomás Ó Crohan, who was born and lived his life on the Blasket

A fine example of the traditional Irish long house on Aran. Deep set windows, whitewashed stone walls and securely roped thatch are all features which reflect the influence of the environment and the use of local materials.

THE THATCHER

Bespoke for weeks, he turned up some morning
Unexpectedly, his bicycle slung
With a light ladder and a bag of knives.
He eyed the old rigging, poked at the eaves.

Opened and handled sheaves of lashed wheat-straw.
Next, the bundled rods: hazel and willow
Were flicked for weight, twisted in case they'd snap.
It seemed he spent the morning warming up:

Then fixed the ladder, laid out well honed blades
And snipped at straw and sharpened ends of rods
That, bent in two, made a white-pronged staple
For pinning down his world, handful by handful.

Couchant for days on sods above the rafters
He shaved and flushed the butts, stitched all together
Into a sloped honeycomb, a stubble patch,
And left them gaping at his Midas touch.

Seamus Heaney

Islands, Co. Kerry, describes other problems which a thatched roof can cause:

"The thatch would have been all right if the hens would only have let it alone, but they wouldn't. As soon as the rushes began to decay, and worms could be found in them, a man with a gun couldn't have kept the hens away from scratching and nesting there. Then the drips would begin, and a dirty drip it was too, for there was too much soot mixed with it. The hens nested so deep in the thatch that the women often lost them, for a hen wouldn't even answer the call to food when she was broody. The little lasses very often brought a hatful or a capful of eggs down from the houses. The children made a mess of the thatch too, always hunting for eggs. It was as good as a day at Puck Fair to listen to two of the women whose houses adjoined, quarrelling with one another about the ownership of the eggs."

DÍON SÚGÁN – ROPED THATCH

As we have seen, the usual material for thatching in Aran is rye-straw. It is tough and hardy and has quite a long life. Before a roof is thatched, a thin layer of rough grass (or, in areas more fertile than Aran, heather sods) is fixed over the roof timbers. This forms a sound base for the thatch.

The thatcher first spreads a layer of straw, about 10 cm. thick, along the eaves at the base of the roof. Then he spreads another layer above this, overlapping the first; and so on until he reaches the roof-ridge.

When he has finished one side, the thatcher starts at the bottom of the other side, and works his way up the ridge again. Finally, a quantity of straw is spread evenly over the ridge.

The new roof is now ready to be secured. The thatcher stretches long pieces of grass rope *súgán* over the roof ridge at intervals of about 30 cms. These are fixed to wooden or stone pegs set into the wall beneath the eaves. Sometimes, where there are no pegs, the rope is tied to heavy stones which hang over the eaves and weigh down the thatch. Other pieces of rope are then fixed crosswise, sometimes all over the thatch, sometimes just at the ridge and eaves, and fastened to pegs set into the gable walls.

The rope forms a heavy net over the thatch and keeps it in place. When the thatcher wants to renew the thatch, he first removes the old rope. The rope is made by the people of the house helped by friends and neighbours. Here, Synge describes how the

Roped Thatch, (in Irish Díon Súgán)

people twist the straw together to make the rope:

"In our own cottage the thatching — it is done every year — has just been carried out. The rope-twisting was done partly in the lane, partly in the kitchen when the weather was uncertain. Two men usually sit together at this work, one of them hammering the straw with a heavy block of wood, the other forming the rope, the main body of which is twisted by a boy or girl with a bent stick specially formed for this employment.

In wet weather, when the work must be done indoors, the person who is twisting recedes gradually out of the door, across the lane, and sometimes across a field or two beyond it. A great length is needed to form the close network which is spread over the thatch, as each piece measures about fifty yards. When this work is in progress in half the cottages of the village, the road has a curious look, and one has to pick one's steps through a maze of twisting ropes that pass from the dark doorways on either side into the fields.

When four or five immense balls of rope have been completed, a thatching party is arranged, and before dawn some morning they come down to the house, and the work is taken in hand with such energy that it is usually ended within the day.

Like all work that is done in common on the island, the thatching is regarded as a sort of festival. From the moment a roof is taken in hand there is a whirl of laughter and talk till it is ended, and, as the man whose house is being covered is a host instead of an employer, he lays himself out to please the men who work with him.

The day our own house was thatched the large table was taken into the kitchen from my room, and high teas were given every few hours. Most of the people who came along the road turned down into the kitchen for a few minutes, and the talking was incessant."

INSIDE THE COTTAGE

The centre of every Aran home is the hearth which is set at ground level in the stone flagged kitchen. The fire is kept alight constantly, both in summer and in winter. At night, ashes are piled over the burning sods to keep the embers glowing until morning. The fire sits at floor level on iron rods with a shallow pit underneath into which the ashes can fall. A wide chimney breast juts out from the wall, creating a large recess on either side of the fire. Many hearths have a stone bench built into this recess which provides a warm seat for an old or ailing member of the family.

An iron 'crane' stands at one side with a jib extending over the back of the fire. Several hooks hang from this and the woman of the house suspends the kettle and cast-iron cooking pots on them. Sods of turf are placed on the fire with iron tongs and the stone flags around the hearth are swept with a small bundle of twigs tied together for this purpose.

Many cottages have a *cleibhí,* a small square cubby hole, set in to the wall of the hearth. Pipes, tobacco, and perhaps tea, are kept in these, ready for use when required.

TURF

Though the islands have an extremely heavy rainfall, surface water drains off quickly and percolates down through the many cracks in the limestone pavements. Peat has never had the opportunity to form on this dry surface and the islanders are severely handicapped by the absence of bogs where they could cut and 'save' their own fuel. All turf used on the islands has to be bought and hookers cross over from the Connemara mainland with regular loads of 'saved' turf. As many as fifteen hookers may come on a particular day and the islanders unload the fuel and pay for it, usually in cash, but sometimes by bartering a calf or bullock with the suppliers.

FURNITURE

Houses on Aran are small and some structures basically consist of a single room. Space is precious and the furniture strictly functional — small chairs, a table, a dresser, beds, a wooden chest for storage and a long bench-seat which stands against the back wall.

Tomás Ó Crohan of the Blasket Islands writes about the house he grew up in, typical of the island dwellings of the 1870's and 1880's:

"The tables used in the little houses were rather like a kneading trough — a board with a raised frame round it to keep in the potatoes or anything else they put on them, and a stand of tripod shape that could be folded up so that the stand and the kneading trough could be hung up on the wall till they were needed.

We had bowls and plates in every house, wooden mugs, a chair or two, and a few stools. The chairs had seats of twisted rope made of hay or straw. There was a pot-rack of iron in every house, and still is, to hang things on over the fire, and there was a pair of tongs of some sort or other on the hearth.

They have cups and saucers in every house now and a full dresser, making a fine show."

The sleeping area, in such a house, is usually not large enough for the whole family, so some members may sleep in the kitchen on a settle-bed — a simple bedstead of wood which can be doubled up to form a high backed bench by day. In other instances, a family may keep a bed upright against the kitchen wall and tip it down when it is needed at night.

LIGHTING

Candles and oil lamps, supplied from the mainland, provide light for the houses at night. When sharks were more plentiful, their oil, or that of seals or even that of fish such as scad and pollock, was burned with a straw or rush wick in a home-made lamp called a cresset.

Tomás Ó Crohan describes these lamps as used on his island around 1880:

"The cresset was a little vessel, shaped like a boat or canoe, with one or two pointed ends, three or four feet to it, and a little handle or grip sticking out of its side — the whole thing about eight or ten inches long. The fish or seal oil was put into it, the reed or wick was dipped in the oil and passed over the pointed end of the cresset, and as it burnt away, it was pushed out. The pith of the rush formed the wick, and often they used a soft twine of cotton or linen for it. They would often use a large shell instead of a cresset for a light. I don't remember at what date paraffin came in. A fragment of turf or a chip of bog-deal was the older fashion, I used to hear them say."

FOOD AND DRINK

Potatoes are an essential part of an Aran family's diet. They are eaten in quantity for 'dinner', the main meal, taken at mid-day in most homes. They are boiled in their jackets in a large round bottomed iron pot which is suspended from a hook over the fire. When cooking is complete the pot is stood on its cast iron legs at one side of the fire and the potatoes transferred to a plate, or, in some cases, a shallow wicker basket. Potatoes are flavoured with salt and butter and milk is usually consumed with the meal. Other food such as salt fish, may be cooked or stewed with the potatoes.

Fresh meat is usually eaten only when a farmer kills one of his sheep or pigs. On such occasions he will share the meat with neighbouring families. Bacon, which is home cured, is the most frequently eaten meat. At certain festive times of the year, such as Christmas and Easter, a family may eat one of their chickens or geese.

A limited variety of vegetables is produced for home consumption. Families may grow some onions and cabbage in a small 'garden' near the dwelling house. Cabbage is the most popular vegetable and is frequently eaten with boiled bacon. It may also be mixed with potatoes and onions in a dish called 'colcannon'.

Colcannon should correctly be made with kale, but is more often made with cabbage. A plain gold ring, a sixpence, a thimble or a button are often put into the mixture. The ring means you will be married within a year; the sixpence denotes wealth, the thimble a spinster and the button a bachelor. The following is a common recipe:

1 lb. each of kale or cabbage, and potatoes, cooked separately
2 small leeks or green onion tops
1 cup milk or cream
4 oz. (½ cup) approx. butter
Salt, pepper and a pinch of mace

Have the kale or cabbage cooked, warm and well chopped up while the potatoes are cooking. Chop up the leeks or onion tops,

while the potatoes are cooking. Chop up the leeks or onion tops, green as well as white, and simmer them in milk or cream to just cover, until they are soft. Drain the potatoes, season and beat them well; then add the cooked leeks and milk.

Finally blend in the kale, beating until it is a pale green fluff. Do this over a low flame and pile it into a deep warmed dish. Make a well in the centre and pour in enough melted butter to fill up the cavity. The vegetables are served with spoonfuls of the melted butter. Any leftovers can be fried in hot bacon fat until crisp and brown on both sides.

White and brown wheaten flour, and yellow maize flour, must be delivered from the mainland. Bread dough is mixed using skimmed milk and bread soda and the bread is baked in a pot-oven. The pot-oven is a straight-sided, flat-bottomed iron pot which sits on a bed of embers at the side of the fire. The dough is placed in the pot, and the iron lid covered with glowing turf-sparks. The dough is thus heated from both bottom and top and is baked slowly and evenly. The pot-oven can also be used for roasting fresh meat or fresh fish such as ray.

Milk and tea are drunk in every home. Buttermilk left over after churning, is a refreshing, if sharp, occasional drink. Water for tea is boiled in a heavy iron kettle suspended from the fire crane. It is customary to keep a kettle "on the boil" in between mealtimes so that tea can be brewed for anyone who calls.

CLOTHES

The men wear trousers and waistcoats of homespun tweed, grey or light-brown in colour. Under the waistcoat they wear a woollen sweater or 'gansey' which may be a natural off-white colour or, sometimes, dyed dark blue. A brightly coloured belt called a crios may be tied around the waist and knitted socks and hand-made cowhide slippers called 'pampooties' are the usual footwear. An Aran man wears a knitted cap, seldom removed except at church and at mealtimes.

Women normally wear calf-length red or dark hand-woven skirts and knitted sweaters and they don headscarves or brightly coloured shawls when going out-of-doors. Like the men they wear pampooties and black woollen stockings.

Both boys and girls wear long dark coloured petticoats of wool, even when they have commenced school, lowering the hem as they grow. Later they wear a scaled down version of the adult dress. They go barefoot in summer.

SPINNING AND WEAVING

Wool is the principal material used by the island women in the making of the family's clothing. Their own sheep supply most of the wool which is spun in the home and sent to the local weaver who produces the cloth on a hand loom. From this cloth trousers, waistcoats and skirts are made, often by a travelling tailor who lives with each family while completing their order.

In this passage a visitor talks to an island woman who is engaged in spinning wool for her family's clothing:

'Passing the open door of a cottage one afternoon and catching a glimpse of a spinning wheel turning merrily, I paused for a moment to watch. The woman of the house, looking up, saw me and invited me in.

I felt as if I had slipped right into the middle of an old story as I sat down on a low stool by the fire. The spinning wheel, mounted on a low stand, dominated the small kitchen, and on the floor beside it was a heap of fleecy wool in soft, loose strands.

Taking a strand of wool, the woman held it beside the end of spun wool on the bobbin, then with her other hand she began turning the wheel.

"Whirr," away it went, and "birr" sang the shuttle merrily, while in and out she pulled the thread like elastic, bent down for another strand, and "whirr" it went again.

" 'Tis in a hurry I am," she told me, "to get it spun the way the weaver can be making a bit of flannel for me."

"You have a weaver on the island?" I asked.

"Oh, faith and we have, he lives up beyond there." *Birr* sang the shuttle.

"Would you like to be trying a hand at it yourself?" she asked. "Let you hold it like that," she showed me, as I took a strand of fleece and began to turn the wheel.

The thread broke. She mended it, and I tried again. This time the wool flew into a tangled mess on the shuttle, much to the amusement of the two children who had just come in from school.

"I'll make it all right," their mother said comfortingly, and I stood by like a little girl learning knitting, who has handed a mess of dropped stitches to her mother to be picked up.

"I'm afraid now it is the sack you would be getting and you trying to spin," she said, as she took it from me and deftly spun

Wool from the Aran sheep drying, having been washed and carded. The housewife will spin the wool into yarn which a local weaver will weave into cloth. The housewife, or a travelling tailor, will make the family's clothes from this cloth.

A spinning wheel used in island homes to make woollen yarn and knitting wool. In the background is the open dresser and delph, typical furniture of the Aran kitchen. In the left background is a large wooden chest used as a dry store for flour and oatmeal.

out the tangle.

When the bobbin was full, she brought over a ball of wool fit for a giantess to knit with, nearly seven pounds she said it weighed. It filled her whole wide red petticoat lap as she sat down and wound on the newly-spun thread, while a little girl held the bobbin.

When spun it looked a dirty greyish colour, but when washed she told me it comes up "white as the waves and them breaking."

Then she showed me another gigantic ball, this time of dark brown wool, the natural colour of the fleece from the dark sheep.

"Them two together makes a nice bit of cloth; wait a minute now and I'll show you a bit."

She brought over one of the sleeveless coats which the Aran men wear over their knitted jerseys. It was navy blue at the back, and this brown and white tweed in the front.

"It is how the women are the tailors on this island," she said; "we make everything, even the trousers."

"Then it is all home industry, right from the sheep-rearing to the clothesmaking?"

"All except the carding. We send the wool to Galway the way they would be carding it for us. The old women used to do that themselves, too, but it was heavy work surely, and half the night the poor things would be busy at it. It comes lighter on us now, though faith and it is hard enough."

"And what about the jerseys, do you knit them yourselves?" — for I had already admired the work of many of them — beautifully knitted they are, in elaborate patterns of ropes and trailing sprays.

"Faith and we do, every one of them; and dye the wool ourselves, too, with indigo dye, the stuff that would turn you out of the kitchen with the smell that's in it. And it is several days it must stay there in the pot; but when 'tis done, sure heaven and earth would be unable to move the colour that would be in it. Though indeed there is many would rather use the new dyes now, for it is a lot easier they are. But they are not near as good. With a dropeen of rain on them the dye comes off, and it is blue you would be underneath, and I'm thinking that can't be good for anyone, surely."

"And what about the red petticoats; how do you dye them?" I asked.

"Oh, it is the same way with them. It used to be all the old madder dye, but now it is the cheap red dyes they are getting from Galway, and I am thinking it is a pity. Ah, sure the whole world is changing; I don't know what is coming over things at all."

She, too, like everyone else, complained of the wet turf. The fire, instead of burning with a red glow, was all smouldering smoke, much of which came puffing out in clouds into the kitchen. Days and months of turf smoke had stained the white-washed chimney-piece a rich tobacco brown, and mellowed the old rafters. Above the chimney hung two bunches of cow-hide cut into squares ready to make pampooties.

Reluctantly I said good-bye, for I had stayed a long time fascinated by the whirr of the wheel and the talk of the woman as she turned it.'

KNITTING

Whereas the women of the islands have knitted their families' sweaters and stockings for centuries, the knitting of the 'Aran' sweater, with its intricate patterns of stitching was introduced to the islands only after the famine, as a means of creating cash employment. The 'sculptured' ornate sweaters quickly became part of every islander's clothing, and each family acquired its own distinctive combination of stitches. The patterns of the sweaters and stockings have been used to identify bodies recovered from the sea. The Aran women are remarkably proficient at this 'traditional' style of knitting and, working from memory, can rapidly create lines of stitches in a myriad of changing sequences.

THE CRIOS

Weaving the brightly coloured tie-belts is another distinctive craft practised by the islanders. The weaver makes a skein from lengths of different coloured wool. He holds the skein taut by placing one looped end around his neck and passing his foot through the other. Shuttle-like his hand is passed in and out through the strands, trailing coloured wools, and creating a variety of radiant designs. When the weaving of the crios is finished, the strands of wool at either end are plaited into long tassels. The wearer winds the crios several times round his waist and knots the ends together.

PAMPOOTIES

Pampooties are the light cowskin footwear of the Aran Islanders.

The cow hide is cleaned and hung on the kitchen wall or on the rafters until required. J. M. Synge was given a pair of these shoes by the family he lodged with, and had to learn how to walk in them. Here is his account of the incident:

'Michael walks so fast when I am out with him that I cannot pick my steps, and the sharp-edged fossils which abound in the limestone have cut my shoes to pieces.

The family held a consultation on them last night, and in the end it was decided to make me a pair of pampooties, which I have been wearing today among the rocks.

They consist simply of a piece of raw cowskin, with the hair outside, laced over the toe and round the heel with two ends of fishing-line that work round and are tied above the instep.

In the evening, when they are taken off, they are placed in a basin of water, as the rough hide cuts the foot and stocking if it is allowed to harden. For the same reason the people often step into the surf during the day, so that their feet are continually moist.

At first I threw my weight upon my heels, as one does naturally in a boot, and was a good deal bruised, but after a few hours I learned the natural walk of man, and could follow my guide in any portion of the island.

In one district below the cliffs, towards the north, one goes for nearly a mile jumping from one rock to another without a single ordinary step and here I realized that toes have a natural use, for I found myself jumping towards any tiny crevice in the rock before me, and clinging with an eager grip in which all the muscles of my feet ached from their exertion.'

BASKET-MAKING

Basket making is yet another of the crafts with which the islander must supply his everyday needs. Panniers for the donkey's back, storage baskets for turf and potatoes, dish-baskets for cooked potatoes and 'spillet' baskets for the fisherman's long lines are all made from the willow shoots, known locally as 'sally' which are grown in little groves about the island.

Basket making is a traditional craft which makes use of local material. The 'sallies', or willow rods, are grown in damp hollows around the islands. Baskets are used for carrying potatoes and turf, as a 'reel' for long-lines and as panniers for donkeys and horses.

Uprights are planted in the ground and a 'wall' is created by weaving lighter rods in and out between these uprights. The basket may be deep or shallow, rectangular, circular, or semi-circular, and trimmed with one or more handles depending on its function.

specíal occasíons

CÉILÍ IS A GATHERING OF NEIGHBOURS and relatives for an evening's enjoyment and it usually involves music, dancing and story-telling as well as eating and drinking. The occasion for holding a *ceílí* may be a wedding in the family, the return of an emigrant or simply the celebration of a festive time of the year. The *céilí* is held in the kitchen and adjoining room of the cottage. A barrel of stout is set up in the corner of the kitchen and one man is delegated to 'pull' the drink for the evening. Whiskey may also be provided, particularly for the old men who sit about the fire reminiscing on their young days. Poteen, illicit spirit distilled from grain, may be imported from the Connemara mainland for the occasion. The older women congregate in the room beside the kitchen where they enjoy a quiet chat while keeping an eye on the proceedings. Here, too, a table is set with food and the gathering is seated in shifts.

The musicians take their place in the corner of the kitchen and the man of the house ensures that their glasses are never empty. The fiddle and the accordion are the instruments most frequently played but the tin whistle, uileann pipes and fife or concert flute sometimes supply the music. A good musician is widely respected; his repertoire of tunes is a cherished hoard passed down through the bow strings of a long line of creative performers. Mainland musicians, particularly those from Co.Clare, are sometimes invited to play. In a crisis, when an instrumentalist can't be found, music is supplied by a lilter who reproduces the rhythms of the dance tune, varying a limited number of syllables with a suitable sound pattern.

SINGING

Solo singing is usually unaccompanied. Long lilting ballads tell of love and emigration and old sorrows. This style of singing, known as *sean nós,* involves difficult grace notes and flourishes. A good singer requires technical skill as well as the ability to interpret the emotions of the song. The audience listens attentively to the singer, interrupting at the end of a verse with a murmured word of encouragement, such as *Dia leat* or *Dia go deo leat.*

HOUSE-WALKING

A more frequent, and less formal, feature of social intercourse is the nightly visits of individuals to their neighbours' houses especially in the winter. The male members of the family engage in this while the women usually remain in their own homes. The men may sit and talk around the fire while smoking a pipe, or, in designated houses, play cards or listen to a *seanchaí.* They usually depart long before midnight. During the summer fishing season, if the sea is too rough for fishing, the men may congregate at the pier head or near the curragh stands and enjoy the sunshine as they talk.

MASS TIME

Sunday mornings offer an opportunity to both men and women to socialise and converse with their neighbours. People like to dress up in their best clothes and the women and girls bring out a special shawl kept for such occasions. The men and older boys walk to church on their own, the women and young children not usually appearing with husband or father. In church, men sit on the left hand side, women on the right, and after Mass, they leave the church grounds, or stand around chatting in groups, with members of their own sex.

MARRIAGE

Marriages on the islands are arranged with the general consent of the young couple and their parents. An uncle or adult friend of either family may conduct the bargaining which involves mutual agreement on the amount of the dowry which the bride's father will give her. The young couple have, of course, a considerable say in the matter and in most cases are well known to each other before any approach is made. Here, Tomás Ó Crohan, tells of how his family 'made' a match for him and he stresses the considerations which influenced their final choice.

'One night after I'd been out — and it was pretty late on in the night, too — whom should I find in the house when I came in but windy Diarmid, and his voice was going as loud as ever I'd heard it; he was getting at the old couple, explaining what an unhandy thing it'd be for them if they spent another year without a soul to help them — "and maybe two years," says he; "and I've got a proposal for you from the best girl that ever broke bread, the finest and the handsomest girl every way."

They didn't break off the talk after I came in, and we kept it up till you'd have thought that everybody in the house was in complete agreement; though the whole affair was to be gone into again, for all the advisers were not present. Be that as it may, Diarmid went out, and he could have trodden on a shell-less egg without breaking it. He fancied that the bargain was sealed.

My sister Maura, who had been in America and who had come back home and married again, heard that Diarmid the rake had been in our house with a match on his hands, and she came to see if there was any truth in the story. We told her how things stood, and she didn't like the idea at all; she made it plain to the old couple what a responsibility anyone was taking on himself if he didn't marry near home, but made an alliance with a family that lived a long way off and wouldn't be in a position to lend a hand on a rainy day.

She had herself marked down an excellent knowledgeable girl, whose people lived in the village, so that they could lend us a hand when we needed it, and she went on to explain the whole affair to us, like a woman reciting a litany, till she had the whole lot of us as tame as a cat.

She'd always had a great hankering after her first husband's people, and his brother's daughter it was that she'd marked down for us.'

Such marriages are generally successful when there is mutual goodwill and respect present. The wedding is an occasion for lavish hospitality and general celebration, the ceremony taking place shortly after the match is made. Early spring is the preferred season as it is not possible to have a marriage solemnised with nuptial Mass during Lent. Weddings may also take place in early summer but an autumn wedding is frowned upon. The islanders

like to say "what is bound in Autumn is loosed in the Spring".
Here is an account of a marriage ceremony and the *bainis*
(wedding feast) which followed:

'Upon invitation of a cousin of a bride-to-be, we attended the
wedding of a young couple of Onaght, a village at the far end of
Inishmore. The ceremony took place in a chapel midway of the
island.

When we arrived the building was already filled with kneeling
friends, with a swarm of tufted-topped boys and young men
occupying the choir and leaning far forward so as to miss nothing.
The bride and bridegroom knelt at the altar rail, with an attendant
at each side. The wedding ring reposed on the rail, on top of two
silver half-crowns, which seemed to be the fee.

The service was in Irish, except for the Latin ritual. It was all
very simple and solemn and as soon as it was over the guests
poured out for the beginning of the fun, while the man and wife
withdrew to sign the register.

Persons of all ages now thronged the roadway below the church.
Women and girls had clambered onto half a dozen jaunting cars,
and men and boys had mounted, two and even three together, to
the bare backs of horses.

Other guests, perhaps not so close to the happy union, were
prepared to walk the three-mile stretch to the new home. But
there was no hurry about starting.

A fiddler arrived and the dance was on. One after another the
young men volunteered, or responded to calls, and showed their
prowess on the hard earth of the road, while the crowd kept time
and cheered. We found the 24-hour jubilee in full blast. A
concertina had been added to the orchestra and a second and a
third fiddler appeared later. Into a kitchen of not more than
twelve by fourteen feet fully sixty persons had crowded in the
form of a hollow square, with space in the middle for four
dancers. Here old and young couples were succeeding each other
in jigs and reels, and the old seemed equally accomplished and
more persistent. The light was dim because the door was low and
the two windows small. The August day was warm for the Arans,
and a mingled odor of turf smoke and moist woolens pervaded the
room.

In the adjacent bedchamber, toward which I wedged my way
behind the hospitable bridegroom, tea was being served, together
with broken loaves and cake.'

DEATH

Death to the islander is an accepted part of the condition of living. As in rural Ireland generally, a corpse is 'waked' in the house until it is taken to the church on the afternoon of the day following the death.

Friends and neighbours gather to pay their respects to the dead person and to condole with the family. On entering the house a caller kneels by the bed where the corpse is laid out and prays briefly. Sympathy is offered to members of the immediate family and the caller joins the other mourners in the kitchen.

The reponse to an individual's death is related to the circumstances. If the death was sudden and tragic, as in the case of a young man drowned at sea or a mother with young children dying at childbirth, the mourners spend the night consoling and supporting the relatives. If, on the other hand, the deceased has been old, or ailing for a long time, the wake is looked on as a meeting of friends. The dead person will be praised, his merits recalled and stories related concerning his skill as farmer or fisherman. Drink will be distributed to the mourners and the atmosphere of the wake house will reflect an optimistic acceptance of the fact of death rather than a sense of irretrievable loss.

In some cases a *Caoine* may be sung — a mourning verse which consists of expressions of loss and sorrow repeated at length in a subdued voice which rises to a loud moan occasionally. Certain old women are regarded as expert 'keeners' and may be found keeping vigil beside the corpse at all wakes in their neighbourhood.

The attendance at a wake reflects the esteem and affection in which a deceased person was held by the community. The family are deeply honoured by a good turn out and will reciprocate the gesture to each of the mourners when the occasion arises.

Tomás Ó Crohan writes about the tragic death of his eldest son. He exemplifies the islanders' acceptance of tragedy and mourning as part of their lot.

'At the time when the young birds come and are beginning to mature, the lads used to go after them. My eldest boy and the King's son planned to go to a place where they were likely to get a young gull — for one of those would often live among the chickens in a house for a year and more.

The two went together after the nests to bring a pair or so of the birds home with them. They were in a bad place, and, as my boy was laying hold of the young gull, it flew up and he fell down the cliff, out on the sea, God save the hearers! He remained afloat on the surface for a long time until a canoe going after lobsters came up and took him aboard.

His grandfather (his mother's father) was in the canoe that took him in. We had only one comfort − there was no wound or blemish anywhere on his body, though it was a steep fall from the cliff. We must endure it and be content! It was a great solace to me that he could be brought ashore and not left to the mercy of the sea. This was the first beginning, and an ill one it was, God help us!

This happened about the year 1890, just when the boy was developing and beginning to lend a hand. Well, those that pass cannot feed those that remain, and we, too, had to put out our oars again and drive on.'

SPECIAL FESTIVALS

In the Aran islands, the Christian festivals of Easter and Christmas are observed with great celebration as are the holy days of important local and national saints. The islanders also celebrate special festivals which are closely associated with the fertility of the land and which probably originated in pre-Christian times. These festivals are celebrated by rural communities, not alone in Ireland, but all over Europe, wherever the cycle of crop growth dominates the pattern of work.

The festivals have Christian names but the rituals are almost the same as in the Celtic era.

ST. BRIGID'S DAY (February 1st)

St. Brigid's Day signals the beginning of the year's work on the farm. Crosses made of straw, which in Celtic times symbolised the sun but are now called St. Brigid's crosses, are placed on the inner side of the thatched roof to protect the family during the coming year. The accumulation of crosses over the years indicates the age of many old houses. Young boys may visit neighbouring houses carrying a straw effigy (meant to represent St. Brigid) and be rewarded with a small gift. A loaf of bread, or a potato, is some-times placed on the doorstep to keep hunger away from the house during the year.

Men and women at Kilronan, 1890. The men wear the home-spun woollen trousers and waistcoat, with knitted 'ganseys' and caps. The women wear the petticoats and multi-coloured shawls of the islands.

MAY DAY (May 1st)

May 1st is the first day of summer. A green branch is brought into the house and kept there throughout the season. The song *Thugamar féin an Samradh Linn* ("We have brought the summer with us") is associated with this custom. Great care is taken on May Eve and May Day to ensure that cattle, butter and water will be unharmed by malevolent fairies or spirits. Some people consider that weather and cloud patterns on May Day are an indication of how the harvest will fare.

ST. JOHN'S EVE (June 23rd)

The Christian churches celebrate the feast of St. John but this date also corresponds with the ancient festival of Midsummer. Bonfires blaze in many villages throughout Ireland and lighted branches from these fires may be thrown into the fields where crops are growing in order to bring good luck. Cattle are driven between two bonfires to ensure that their calves will be healthy.

SAMHAIN (November 1st)

Hallowe'en, the eve of All Saint's Day, corresponds with an ancient feast to commemorate the dead. The spirits of the dead are believed to wander abroad on this night. People remain at home, special games are played and bread is thrown against the door to banish hunger during the coming winter.

the family

HE FAMILY IS THE MOST IMPORTANT social unit on the islands. Together, the members of the immediate or nuclear family form a labour force to carry out the regular duties in the home and on the farm. Large families are regarded as a blessing in Aran and households with ten, twelve, or even more children are not uncommon. But all of these children will not live to reach adulthood. Infant mortality, distance from medical aid and the hazards of the fisherman's work, will ensure that some of them will precede their parents to the grave.

Childlessness is regarded as a misfortune to which there are few parallels. Therefore, when a marriage has taken place, conception and childbirth are anxiously awaited by both the young couple and their parents. The successful birth of a healthy child is an occasion of great joy as it means a continuation of the family name on the land.

Children are named with care and pride. Local national saints' names, such as Enda, Coile (Coley), Gobnait and Patrick are popular and will be found repeated in each succeeding generation of a particular family. Because so many children are named for their grandparents, or for an aunt or uncle, confusion is inevitable and many of the islanders share the same christian names and surnames. The individuals in such cases are distinguished by nicknames derived from the christian names of their fathers and grandfathers. For example, Tomás Ó Flatharta, the son of Paidi Ó Flatharta may be known as Tomás Phaidi to distinguish him from others of the same name. In cases where a woman inherits land and her husband is landless the children will receive a maternal nickname. Seán Ó Sé, the son of Maire and Paidi will in such a case be known as Seán Mhaire.

The 1901 census records show that a total of 61 different surnames were represented on the islands but certain names such as Flaherty, Conneely and Dirrane occurred much more frequently than others.

HEAD OF THE FAMILY

The father is usually the dominant member of the family and is regarded by outsiders as representing the whole family. The farm is known by his name and the farm house and most of the goods descend from father to son along with the patronym. Decisions with regard to farming and fishing are made by the father, though frequently there is informal consultation with the other members of the family.

The mother's sphere of influence is confined to the work of the house and farmyard. The tasks which recur daily are regarded as the province of the woman. These include cooking, washing, cleaning, churning, bread-making, spinning and clothes-making, within the home; and the feeding and care of chickens and other fowl, and perhaps the pigs, within the farmyard. Generally the older boys help the father in his tasks; girls and younger boys are the assistants of the mother and are subject to her discipline.

Even though the father is regarded as the formal head the mother may exert a considerable influence on the family through her management of the home and through her direction of the children. In some instances a woman may be the dominant partner in the family's dealings with the community. This is frowned on by the islanders and an ideal relationship is considered to exist between a couple who are equally competent in their individual tasks and who defer to each other by consultation and display of mutual respect.

THE WOMAN'S ROLE

After marriage the Aran woman tends to merge her identity with that of her husband and her new family. Her interest will focus on the home and she may come to regard outside events as having little bearing on her life. The Aran woman's expectations are largely bound up with the rearing of her family and she derives her main satisfaction from the progress of its members through life. The bonds between parents and children are of an enduring kind and loyalty to family is a quality on which community opinion places great emphasis.

KINSHIP

Many households are comprised of three generations. Paternal grandfathers and grandmothers of the children live in the house and are an integral part of the organisation of daily life. Family structure is not confined to the immediate family group but extends a network of relationships outwards to a larger kin grouping. Every islander belongs to such an extended family grouping, which he or she will refer to as *mo mhuintear*. Great pleasure is taken in reciting lists of cousins and marriage relations and even quite young people display a fascination with their family linkages, showing a consciousness of belonging to this larger group. The kin group provides a support system for the individual and his family. He can confidently call on his kinfold in times of crisis or distress but, even more importantly, he shares his everyday work and leisure with them. They will assist him in the saving of the harvest, the building of a house or the thatching of a roof; they may form part of his curragh crew, or join with him to purchase nets. This system of mutual help and obligation is invaluable, particularly in an area where money is scarce and may be insufficient to hire labour.

This exchanging of labour or 'cooring' will also involve the immediate relatives of a man's spouse, who become members of his and his children's kin groups.

CHANGE IN THE FAMILY

Marriage is a crucial event in Aran family life. The old farmer and his wife give up their title to house and land and retire from active management. The young man and his bride assume control and from then on the farm is regarded as theirs.

Though the old couple remain on in the home it is regarded as desirable that all others should leave in order to present a fair opportunity to the young couple who are starting a new family. Unmarried sons may emigrate, or in some cases, marry and build a house of their own, though without farm property they know that there is little opportunity for them to survive in their own

*Father and son, Kilronan 1890.
The growing boy begins to spend
more and more time in his
father's company learning from
him the skills of farming, and
later, of fishing.*

community. Unmarried daughters may themselves marry and
move to their new husband's home, but the isolated and
numerically limited community offers few partners of suitable
age, many of whom are in any case too closely related to satisfy
the requirements of Church and State. The old parents and the
brother who has assumed ownership will seek to create a good
match for each daughter but many women follow the footsteps
of their bachelor brothers to England and America.

A smooth transition of ownership and control is vital to the
happiness and well-being of all concerned: the old order changes
and a new generation in the family tree is created. Not least, the
kin group, on which the family can rely for mutual aid, is
extended and consolidated through the links with the 'new' wife's
family.

THE KIN GROUP AND EMIGRATION

It is not just in relation to farming and fishing on the islands that the kin group functions. Members of the extended family will maintain the bonds and sense of obligation even when separated by three thousand miles of ocean. Thus children who have emigrated will regularly send gifts of money to their parents in order to assist them in rearing the younger members of the family. Even an aunt or uncle may perform this service, particularly at Christmas time. This inflow of cash is a vital component in the precarious economic balance on which island life depends.

The kin group also forms a channel through which emigration can take place, making the journey to a strange land less hazardous and intimidating. In fact this link has facilitated emigration from the islands since the Famine. An emigrant, whether male or female, plays an important role in making possible the migration of brothers and sisters and even nephews and nieces. Money is sent home for the fare and expenses, a job is sought on behalf of the new immigrant who is cushioned during the first difficult years of exile by a group of relatives and friends.

His native language is of no economic value in his new situation, serving only to isolate him from the mainstream of American life but it helps him and his fellows to preserve their bonds of loyalty and affection in an alien environment and he may continue to use it among friends and relatives from Aran for years after he first emigrates.

Emigration to America in most cases means taking up a permanent home and livelihood in a new country. Both he and his parents know that they will probably never meet again. The finality of separation has something of the anguish associated with death. It is hardly surprising then to find the sending-off gathering for a young emigrant described as an "American Wake". Music, singing and dancing will take place but a more sombre note, almost one of mourning, underlies the gaiety and is never far from the surface of the apparently cheerful gathering.

An emigrant may spend forty or fifty years in the country of his adoption and may die without seeing his native land again but contact with home will usually be maintained, if only by way of the annual card at Christmas.

moᴅeRᴎ aRaᴎ

OME FEATURES OF LIFE on the Aran Islands have undergone little change in the past fifty years but in many respects the way of life made famous by Synge has disappeared forever. The population has continued to decline throughout the twentieth century and emigration has drained the life-blood from the community. Tourism and the mass media have brought the outside world into every Aran home. The most important change of all has been the growth of the islanders' desire to develop their economic resources in order to achieve the standard of living which is taken for granted elsewhere in Ireland.

FARMING

Farming is still important in the island economy but the people are no longer as dependent on it for their livelihood as they were in the past. The spade and the scythe have not been replaced by modern machinery as the Aran farms are too small to allow for the purchase of machinery and the fields too tiny and rocky to allow its use.

The population has declined steadily since the mid-nineteenth century affecting the size and ownership of farms. Frequently, all but one of the children in a particular family emigrated leaving one son at home to manage the land and care for their parents. Should this remaining son not marry, as was often the case, the land passed, on his death, to a nephew or cousin, and was amalgamated with this relative's holding. Thus, the number of farms on the Aran Islands dropped from a total of 373 in 1927 to

349 in 1960. The land which made up the 'vanished' farms was added to other farms and helped to increase the number of holdings containing 20 hectares or more and to bring three farms over the 40 hectares mark. There has been no change in the total number of holdings during the last 17 years.

The Irish Government set up an Interdepartmental Committee, in 1957, to examine the problems facing small farms on the Western Seaboard. This committee concluded that there could be no hope of improving the standard of living of small farmers without bringing about a huge increase in average farm size. They felt that farmers could not possibly make an acceptable living on farms of 12 hectares or less.

The majority of holdings on the Aran Islands are small. Thirty of them are merely one acre potato patches and an additional 173 holdings have less than 12 hectares each. All of these holdings contain tracts of infertile land and bare rock as well as their potato gardens and strips of grazing. Average farm income is very low and most of these farms, could not, even in the most favourable circumstances, yield an adequate family income.

Irish membership of the European Economic Community has made the plight of the small farmer even worse. The Community has plans for developing agriculture in the member countries which involves the phasing out of smaller farms. Under its Mansholdt Plan proposals the majority of Aran farms would be regarded as too small to be developed to a level where they could provide an income comparable to that provided by industrial jobs. In the eyes of the EEC such farms are not qualified to receive grants and loans to increase productivity.

The last fifty years have seen the development of a number of large farms on Aran. The owners of these farms may be able to make a living solely from their land but the future for the average Aran farmer is bleak unless work is created for him in industry, tourism or fishing.

Changes in farm size and in family life style have brought about a number of adjustments in the type of farming activities in which the islanders engage. There has been a general decline in the number of acres of crops planted each year since the beginning of the century. In 1925 a total of 221 hectares of crops were planted but by 1973 this figure had fallen to less than 53 hectares.

The potato is still the most important crop but the number of acres planted has decreased each year. In 1925 a total of 40 hectares of potatoes were grown but this figure had dropped to

New house types have changed the Island landscape. The traditional thatched roof has proved too costly to repair and replace and the skills of masonry have been generally replaced by the use of concrete blocks. The pony and trap is an ideal vehicle in which to tour the islands.

80 hectares by 1960 as the declining population needed to produce less food. Since 1960, however, the potato acreage has rapidly decreased reaching an all time low of 38 hectares in 1973, completely outpacing the continuing population decline. The potato, then, seems to have lost some of its importance as the diet of the islanders became more varied and relied less on the traditional staples. A limited amount of cabbage, turnips and other vegetables are also sown for domestic use.

Corn crops have suffered a similar decline. A total of 58 hectares of rye and just over 1 hectare of oats and barley were planted in 1925. By 1960 the total acreage had dropped to 23 reflecting the decline in the use of rye as a roofing material. Imported roof tiles have proved cheaper to erect and maintain on new houses and many of the older thatched-roof houses have fallen into disrepair as occupants emigrated or died. The manual labour involved in planting, reaping, flailing and winnowing rye, without the aid of machinery, has been another deterrent and may lead, eventually, to the disappearance of the thatched roof from the island landscape. In 1973 only 5 hectares of rye and 5 hectares of oats were planted.

CATTLE

Farmers have moved away from tillage and increasingly devoted their land to cattle rearing. The islander no longer seeks to provide for all the needs of his family but concentrates, rather, on those activities which are most profitable. Cattle prices have risen considerably in the past decade and they received an added boost with Irish entry into the EEC in 1973. The hardy island cattle are popular with buyers as they are easily fattened when grazed on fertile grassland for a few months. Cattle rearing makes for an easier work load and is therefore popular with the many elderly farmers and the younger farmer-fishermen.

Between 1960 and 1973 cattle numbers, on the islands, rose by 40% though there were yearly fluctuations depending on market demand and price. The jobbers come to the monthly fairs on all three islands to bargain for the cattle which, when sold, the farmer undertakes to ship to Galway at his own expense.

Almost all families still keep one or two dairy cows to supply their domestic requirements. Islanders who have no cows buy milk from their neighbours. Bottled milk is sometimes imported during the summer months to satisfy the demand created by the influx of tourists.

A few families still churn milk to make butter for their own use but the practice is in decline and most people buy butter imported from mainland creameries. In 1974 a total of 517 kg. of home-butter was made.

Sheep numbers have declined rapidly in recent years as farmers switched to cattle production. The 1960 total of 2879 sheep had fallen to 465 by 1973 and most of the wool for knitting was imported from the mainland.

Pigs are no longer reared on Aran and the number of poultry has halved in the past 15 years. These and other changes emphasise the passing of self-sufficiency, the concentration on more commercial aspects of farming and the changes in the family diet.

FISHING

The fishing industry in the Aran Islands, as in the rest of Ireland, has had varying fortunes in the years since 1900. The first World War brought a temporary boom to the mackerel fishery but was immediately followed by a period of stagnation and decline. Markets were limited, processing facilities and ice plants were non-existent and the boats and equipment of the Irish fleet could not match those of their foreign competitors. The Irish Sea Fisheries Association was set up by the Government in 1931 to help modernise the industry but the lack of a home market for fish retarded any significant development.

In the last decade, however, the fishing industry has boomed on Aran and the island fleet, based at Kilronan, is one of the finest in the country, employing a total of 85 full time fishermen. This welcome development is a direct result of the work undertaken by the Fisheries Association's successor, Bord Iascaigh Mhara — the Sea Fisheries Board. B.I.M., as it is known, trains fishermen and skippers, helps them to acquire boats, provides port facilities, raises the quality of fish in the market-place through icing and proper handling and promotes the eating of fish among the general public.

The Aran Fleet consists of 21 wooden-hulled boats of 9 metres keel length and upwards. It is based at Kilronan as there is no other pier of suitable size in any of the islands. Six of these boats are large trawlers, nine are medium-sized trawlers and the others are half-decked lobster boats. The boats are owned and crewed by full time fishermen from all three islands. Seventeen Aran men have been trained as skippers on B.I.M. and Fisheries Department courses and are qualified to operate the modern trawlers which Irish boatyards are now producing. A large trawler at present costs from £250,000 to £1,000,000 depending on size and equipment. The purchaser must pay 5% deposit and he receives a grant of 25% of the total cost from B.I.M. and F.E.O.G.A., the EEC development agency. The balance of the cost can be borrowed through B.I.M. at a special interest rate and repaid in regular instalments.

During the 19th century, trawlers depended on sails to propel them but the modern trawler is equipped with a powerful diesel engine. Other equipment includes a winch to pull in the net and a power-block to help lift large catches aboard.

A trawl is a bag-shaped net which is towed over smooth patches of sea bed. The mouth of the net is kept open, vertically, by weighting the ground line and attaching floats to the headline; otter boards (or 'trawl doors') drag the sides of the net outwards. This type of net catches cod, haddock, sole, plaice and other fish which feed on, or near the sea-bed.

A trawl net can also be used to kill shoals of mackerel and herring which swim nearer the surface. Two trawlers, working as a pair, tow the net and thus manage to keep it open without letting it sink to the sea-bed. The larger Aran boats all participate in the herring fishery, travelling to ports all round Ireland in search of shoals. A valuable winter and spring herring fishery has developed in Galway Bay so for part of the year, at least, good catches can be made without having to venture too far from the home port. The herring are lightly salted, or smoked, and exported to the Continent.

The modern trawler is equipped with a range of electronic aids for communication, navigation and fish-finding. It contains comfortable accommodation and cooking facilities for the crew, as the boat may often be at sea overnight. The more recently built boats have centrally heated cabins and a shower room. Trawler men work long and irregular hours and are paid a share of the money realised by the catch rather than a fixed wage. When everything goes well the rewards are good but when fish are scarce, or the weather exceptionally bad, the fisherman may have a very meagre return for his work.

In addition to the trawler fleet, twenty-eight smaller boats, many of them curraghs, work from beaches and small piers in all three islands. They are powered by oars and outboard engines

An 11 metre lobster boat, part of the modern fleet which has transformed the economy of the islands by providing employment for young men who would otherwise have to emigrate. However inflation on the price of new boats has put even relatively small lobster boats beyond the reach of Aran fishermen, who must bear heavier fuel costs and transport costs than the mainland fishermen.

and each is crewed by two or three part-time fishermen who fish with lobster pots and hand lines in summer.

Lobster fishing is carried on in the traditional manner but the modern, wooden-hulled and motor powered boats can handle many more pots and range further from port than the curraghs ever could. Their work is made easier and safer by electronic aids such as the echo-sounder and the radio telephone. The curragh, however, does retain an advantage in that it can be used from Inishmaan and Inisheer where the larger boats would find it difficult to land.

Lobster fishing is a seasonal activity which is dependent on fine weather and calm seas for its success. Lobster and crayfish are delicacies and fetch high prices on the French and Spanish markets but the huge crab catch must be dumped as there is no plant which could process and market them.

The salmon is one of the most valuable fish resources in Aran waters. Each year, in early summer, the mature salmon swim from their feeding grounds in the North Atlantic to their spawning grounds in Irish rivers. But the islanders are prohibited from fishing for salmon, only a few being licensed to catch them with drift nets. A proportion of the salmon must reach the spawning grounds if the species is to survive and, in addition, riverside angling is an important tourist attraction. It is obvious then, that conservation measures are necessary.

Private individuals and companies, though, have legal rights to kill numbers of the fish at the mouths of the rivers. The islanders feel aggrieved that commercial and tourism interests should be catered for while they, isolated as they are from other means of earning a living, are debarred from one of their few potential sources of income. Salmon swim past their island to fuel the mainland economy while emigration continues from Aran and while its inhabitants have to tolerate a standard of living which is lower than that found elsewhere in Ireland.

The rapid development of the fishing industry in the past decade has brought a new prosperity to the Aran islands, particularly to Inishmore, and has done much to halt population decline as young men take to the fishing boat rather than to the emigrant ship. Kilronan pier has recently been improved and the Government has plans to develop Rossaveal, on the Galway mainland, as a convenient landing place for Aran fishermen, as it is only one hour's journey from Inishmore. At present an Aran boat must make a five hour round trip to the Galway docks to land its catch or to refuel. This journey will be eliminated when the new pier at Rossaveal is completed and the harbour dredged to accommodate the larger boats. It is hoped to provide an ice-making plant and a fresh water supply at Rossaveal, where there are already facilities for storing lobsters and processing herring.

But there are major problems which must be solved if the industry is to enjoy further development. The deposit required to buy a new trawler is beyond the means of many young fishermen. Grant and loan facilities are, at present, not available for the purchase of cheap second-hand vessels, even though such boats offer the best opportunity to young men wishing to start out on their own. There are nine qualified skippers working as deckhands in the Aran fleet who could form the basis for the next phase of expansion in the industry.

Fish prices in Ireland are still well below those obtained by the fishermen of other European countries but fuel and gear costs have risen rapidly putting the Irish fisherman at a disadvantage even though he is near to some of the richest fishing grounds in Europe.

But the greatest threat to future prosperity lies in the over-fishing of stocks, particularly by huge fleets of foreign trawlers. The fishermen say that Ireland needs a properly policed "50 mile limit" to its territorial waters within which the boats of other nations would not be allowed to fish. They argue that it is only in such a situation that we can properly conserve stocks and plan the further expansion of the fishing industry.

TOURISM

Tourism is now an important source of income for the Aran Islands. Visitors, from elsewhere in Ireland as well as from other countries, come to the islands in ever-increasing numbers. Some come to learn Irish or improve their command of the language, others to study the unusual geology and flora, or the remarkable collection of ancient remains found on the islands. But the majority come to sample a special way of life, made famous throughout the world by island writers, as well as by a continuous stream of outside writers and artists who have followed in Synge's footsteps to these bare Atlantic rocks where can be found *ciúneas gan uaigneas* – solitude without loneliness.

In recent years an improved schedule of sailings from Galway, and the introduction of regular Aer Arann flights, has increased the number of holidaymakers and day-trippers, particularly in the summer months.

A restaurant has been established at Kilronan and a small hotel has functioned there for some time and many of the families have built extensions on to their houses to accommodate guests. This practice is gradually changing the traditional nature of the islands' homes and family life.

The tourist trade is hindered in its expansion by a number of factors. It can only offer part-time employment and there is frequently an acute shortage of help in the guest houses during the summer high-season. The uncertainty of the piped water supply poses problems for catering, hygiene and sanitation during dry spells. The ever increasing swarms of day-trippers are of little financial benefit to the tourist industry which has not as yet, begun to service this market.

The tourist inspires mixed feelings in the islander. His arrival brings an inflow of money, a rise in employment, albeit seasonal, and an important boost to the self-esteem of the community through the interest shown in, and the value placed on, their way of life.

But the tourist also brings an image of his own way of life with him, an image which is frequently one of material prosperity and urban glamour beside which island life may appear harsh and unpromising to restless young people. Some of the older islanders regret the advent of the tourist, regarding him as one of the reasons for the decline in traditional customs and the language in the Kilronan area, and the continuing migration of young people. Inishmaan and Inisheer have felt less of the impact, in both its positive and negative aspects of tourism. Due to their isolation and difficulties of access they are more liable to attract the language enthusiast than the day tripper.

Inisheer, in particular, benefits from a summer college for students of the Irish language, which attracts large groups of young people from all parts of Ireland to its month-long courses.

OTHER INDUSTRIES

In 1975, a factory was built on Inishmore. It was run by a jewellery company from Birmingham, who employed twelve girls, having sent them to England for training. But this company did not stay long on Aran: and in the summer of 1976 they closed the factory. However, it was soon re-opened by a Dublin based

Modern Aran. Cured sheepskins and traditional Aran knitwear for sale to tourists. Tourism is assuming a major importance in the Aran economy but regretfully, many of the handcrafts sold on the islands are imported and a valuable potential source of employment is ignored.

electronics firm, subsidised by Gaeltarra Eireann. (Gaeltarra Eireann is a State-funded body which seeks to create employment in Gaeltacht areas). A group of young people, some of whom were previously employed in the jewellery plant, are being retrained for this new kind of work. It is hoped that this firm will ultimately employ about 40 people.

Only factories which manufacture small objects made from raw materials which are neither bulky nor perishable could hope to be successful on Aran, as freight costs would otherwise be crippling. The islanders are hopeful that this new venture will survive the many obstacles associated with isolation and distance from markets.

There are some craft shops but these do not only sell goods made on the islands. Some women knit sweaters or weave crioses and sell them to tourists, but this is time-consuming and expensive, as the wool has to be bought and imported from the mainland.

Kelp is no longer burned in Aran, but there are still markets for Aran seaweed. The acid obtained by processing seaweed is used in the preparation of a wide variety of products such as cosmetics and medicines, and the stems of the red seaweed, so plentiful in Aran, are particularly rich in it.

Nowadays the collected weed is shipped to the mainland for processing. Great piles of gathered weed awaiting shipping are a common sight on the piers. However, freight charges are very high and eat into profits made by the sale of seaweed.

HOUSES

The long, low, thatched cottage, so long a feature of the Aran landscape, is no longer the dominant house type. Some of the traditional cottages have been adapted to changing times by the addition of extra rooms and tiled roofs. Many bungalows have been built, similar in design to those found in town and country elsewhere in Ireland. The Department of the Gaeltacht for a time promoted the building of two storey houses, but these are generally agreed to be less suited, than single storey houses, to the climatic conditions found on the islands.

FUEL AND POWER

The Aran Islands have never been connected to the Irish

Inishmaan and Inisheer do not as yet have piers where the Naomh Eanna can land to discharge cargo. A wide range of imported goods are ferried ashore in curraghs. Bottled gas is widely used for cooking and lighting and coal has almost completely replaced turf as a fuel.

POPULATION FIGURES FOR ARAN

Year	Inisheer	Inishmaan	Inishmore	Total
1901	483	421	1,959	2,863
1911	480	420	1,779	2,679
1926	409	380	1,368	2,157
1936	445	375	1,289	2,109
1946	447	388	1,136	1,971
1951	388	361	1,019	1,768
1956	376	361	944	1,681
1961	358	357	933	1,648
1966	345	342	925	1,612
1971	313	319	864	1,496

National Electricity Grid and, until recently, the inhabitants have had to forego the convenience and comfort which the electricity user enjoys. The lack of a cheap, efficient power supply also discouraged industries which might otherwise have come to the islands.

A successful campaign for this basic service resulted in a diesel-engined electricity generator being installed on Inisheer. A similar system began to produce power for Inishmore in December 1975. The Department of the Gaeltacht has now provided a grant of £100,000 to pay for a scheme on Inishmaan, to be completed by summer 1977.

Electricity is expensive, costing about twice as much, per unit consumed, on the islands as it does on the mainland. Co-operatives have had to be set up by the island people to service the generators and maintain supplies, at their own expense, as the national Electricity Supply Board is only responsible for the mainland network. The cost of maintenance is high because materials and skilled labour must be imported. In order to solve this problem the Inishmaan Co-operative has recruited an apprentice diesel fitter who is now undergoing training with AnCO, the Industrial Training Authority.

Turf, coal and paraffin oil are still used as fuel for fires and heating but the cost of these commodities has risen steeply in recent years. Heavy freight charges add further to the cost of turf and coal. The Inishmaan Co-op is now supplying almost all of that island's coal in order to reduce the cost through bulk buying.

WATER SUPPLY

The supply of fresh water, both for domestic use and for farm animals, has always posed a problem in the Aran Islands. Rainfall is adequate but the exposed limestone pavements are permeable and make a very poor water catchment surface. Inishmore now has a water scheme serving all parts of the island. Motor-driven pumps distribute water from the main reservoir, situated on the clifftop near Dún Aengus, to the houses. On the other islands small reservoirs serve groups of houses but many people still must depend on spring wells and rain troughs for their supply. Despite these improvements, water is still scarce on Aran. The islands were badly affected by the recent summer droughts. Water levels in reservoirs were so low that the water supply had to be cut off for a certain number of hours each day.

Water supply remains a problem in the arid limestone landscape. Inishmore now has a water scheme but wells like this are still the only source of supply for many homes on all three islands.

Some time ago, one of the spring-wells on Inishmore was polluted: to fetch water, a man used the drum in which he carried diesel-oil for his tractor. It took a long time before the water in the well was drinkable again. It was the islanders' first experience of water pollution. Now a sign painted on the rock near the well asks its users to keep it clean.

TRANSPORT AND COMMUNICATION

Maintaining contact with the mainland has remained a problem for the islanders. The *Dun Aengus* a sturdy little Dublin-built steamer, initially owned by the Galway Bay Steamship Company, and later by Coras Iompair Eireann (C.I.E.) sailed between Galway and the islands, carrying passengers and cargoes for almost 50 years. In 1958, when she was taken off the route and broken up, she was the oldest steamer in regular service in Western Europe.

She was replaced by the MV *Naomh Eanna,* also Dublin-built, a larger and more efficient steamer. The *Naomh Eanna* runs several times a week all the year round (except during her short annual overhaul).

Passengers being ferried ashore to Inishmaan from the Naomh Eanna. The influx of tourists in the summer months represents a valuable boost to the economy. The introduction of the Aer Arann service of daily flights has been of benefit to islander and tourist alike.

Another vessel, the MV *Galway Bay* sails daily from Galway to Kilronan during the summer, and in the winter when the *Naomh Eanna* is being overhauled. It is also owned by C.I.E.

A privately owned cruiser the *Queen of Aran* sails regularly from Rossaveal on the Connemara coast. This is a short run — it only takes about one hour to sail from Rossaveal to Kilronan. Regular motorboat sailings from Doolin, Co. Clare, to Inisheer are held daily in the summer, and, if the weather is suitable, by request in the winter.

The islanders would like to see a daily scheduled service established and they have approached Government agencies with a view to the setting up of a roll-on roll-off car ferry service. They also feel that the Government should subsidise the transport of goods to the islands as most goods cost 20% — 30% more than they do on the mainland due to high transport costs. It is generally conceded that building materials, being heavy and bulky, are up to 100% more expensive for the prospective housebuilder on the islands of Inishmaan and Inisheer, where there are no suitable piers to accommodate the steamer.

AER ARANN

In 1970 Aer Arann began operating a regular air service between the Aran Islands and Galway. This has done a great deal to improve the islands' contact with the mainland.

Until 1970, all emergencies had been dealt with by the Life Boat Service — patients who had to be taken to mainland hospitals, as well as boats in trouble at sea. The islanders became more and more aware that the service was inadequate. Firstly, the vessel in use was equipped with few navigational aids which meant that any voyage in rough seas or at night was dangerous and lengthy. Secondly, the lifeboat rides at anchor in Kilronan bay and in high seas is very difficult to reach by curragh or rowing boat. Thirdly, money was scarce as the Lifeboat Service was financed completely by voluntary subscriptions. Finally it was a most unsuitable way of bringing emergency medical cases to the mainland — people in need of immediate hospitalisation or surgery and women about to give birth faced a long, cold uncomfortable journey which often caused further complications.

The islanders were determined that this should change, and made their plight known to the national newspapers. One article, which listed the advantages of setting up an island air-service was read by a group of Galway business men, who decided that they would back the plan financially. So, in 1970, Aer Arann, an independent company subsidised by Gaeltarra Eireann was set up.

At first the service just operated between Galway and Killeany in Inishmore. However, since 1973, Inishmaan has also been included in the daily flight schedule. When Inisheer's runway is completed, it will be a three-island service.

The island runways are levelled sand dunes, sown with grass which form a hard dry surface. They have no facilities such as re-fuelling points: the planes are refuelled in Galway.

Aer Arann now has four ten seater (9 passengers and pilot) Britten-Norman "Islander" aircraft on the route. These planes are specially designed for short journeys between islands, and for short take-off and landings. The company employs four pilots and a small staff.

There are daily flights all year round, the frequency on any given day varying with the number of passengers or the amount of freight to be carried.

Aer Arann, more than any other single innovation, has changed the quality of life on the islands as it has bestowed a new freedom of movement on the inhabitants and established much closer contact with the mainland. The islanders feel that Aer Arann deserves a Government subsidy in the form of tax free fuel, similar to the concession already enjoyed by Aer Lingus and C.I.E.

TRANSPORT ON THE ISLANDS

For most people small donkey or horse carts are still the main form of transport on Aran but the number of cars has been increasing on Inishmore, since the first one arrived in 1959. Distances are too short on the other islands for a car to be of any use.

Tractors are used on all three islands; a few each on Inishmaan and Inisheer and a larger number on Inishmore. They are not used, however, for farmwork because the land is too rocky and the fields too small for this to be possible. Instead they are utilised to haul merchandise in from the ferry, or to collect coal and turf from the piers.

Motorbikes are common. The islanders find them useful and economical to run over the short distances. The bicycle is, of course, very useful and popular for travel on the islands. The possession of mechanically propelled vehicles presents problems which do not exist on the mainland. There are no filling stations on the islands, so all petrol and diesel fuel has to be imported in drums. This presents a further difficulty, since, for insurance reasons, the ferry boat will not carry fuel in its hold. The islanders have to find other ways of importing their petrol. Furthermore, cars have to be taken to the mainland or parts have to be brought out to the islands for servicing and maintenance, both operations involving heavy freight charges.

Except for the few tarred "main" roads on Inishmore, roads on Aran are dirt tracks. The car owners complain that the bumpy dirt roads ruin their cars, and the horse and donkey owners complain that the tarred-roads do not give their animals enough grip!

COMMUNICATIONS

Mail arrives from the mainland twice a week and is distributed from the various post-offices — one in Kilronan and one in Kilmurvey on Inishmore, and one each in Inishmaan and Inisheer.

The islands were linked telegraphically to the mainland by submarine cable at the beginning of this century. In the early 1920's the Kilronan telephone exchange was installed but it was not until 1960 and 1961, respectively that Inishmaan and Inisheer got theirs. Private telephones, however, are only common on Inishmore, where there are 10 lines and 72 telephones.

For a long time, the people on Aran have had battery-operated radios, and the establishment of Radio na Gaeltachta (an Irish language radio service) in 1972 has made available a greater number of broadcasts in the Irish language. Many homes now also have television sets.

EDUCATION

All three islands have had their own primary schools since the end of the nineteenth century but until recently those wishing to avail of secondary education have had to attend boarding schools on the mainland with the aid of a special scholarship scheme for Gaeltacht children. Such an education, however, prepared the children for a range of job opportunities which were available only in mainland towns and cities.

A Vocational school was established at Kilronan in 1954 providing courses which are more likely to equip a young person to occupy a place within the local economy. The school is co-educational and at present there are seven full-time teachers and seventy students. Students from Inishmaan and Inisheer lodge with families on Inishmore and return home only at weekends. The school has now developed to include a senior section and students wishing to pursue a Leaving Certificate course no longer have to attend a mainland boarding school.

A full range of subjects are taught, with the exception of metalwork, for which there are no facilities at present. The principal teacher would also like to introduce a building construction course, in the near future. As there are only two builders on the islands there is a need for such a course and it would undoubtedly prove popular with adults as well as with the regular students.

JOB PROSPECTS

Job prospects have improved for boys with the development of the fishing industry. Young people, who have left the islands during the last decade, are now returning to work on local trawlers. The Inishmore factory can only employ a limited number and the guesthouses provide work which is, of its nature, seasonal and temporary. Many girls must still leave in search of employment and most will eventually marry in the mainland and settle permanently there.

LEISURE

The young have a range of leisure pursuits available to them on Inishmore. Céilís and film shows are held in the parish hall on a weekly basis throughout the year and more frequently in summer. The youth club, based in the school, and the public house pool table cater for various groups and a local committee arranges football matches and other sporting events. Almost all of the homes have a radio and many are acquiring television sets now that electricity is available. However, the traditional housewalking continues to some extent, even today.

The Pattern or Patrún, is the great social event of the year. In the past it was customary to visit the holy places on the islands or to travel to the mainland to pray at shrines and holy wells on Pattern day. Nowadays the focus is on sporting competitions. Curragh races are held and are the subject of intense rivalry between crews from each 'village'. Tug-o-war competitions, bicycle races, children's sports and dancing are popular on all three islands.

THE LANGUAGE

Irish remains the everyday language of the Aran Islands despite the ever-increasing contact with the English-speaking mainland through tourism and the mass media. Nowadays, though, many islanders, especially those who live on Inishmore and Inisheer, are bilingual.

For a time, in the 1950's and 1960's the future of Irish, as the first language of the islands, seemed to be in doubt. Many of the young people were leaving to go to English-speaking schools or to work in English-speaking areas, and Kilronan, the most anglicised village of the islands, was beginning to spread its influence to other areas.

In recent years, however, the islanders have become more hopeful that the language will survive. The Vocational School and the thriving fishing industry are attracting people from exclusively Irish speaking places to Kilronan and many of the Kilronan people are going back to the habit of speaking Irish. More and more young men and women are choosing to stay on the islands and Irish is no longer seen as being merely the language of the old. The establishment of Radio na Gaeltachta, the Irish language broadcasting service, has meant that the islanders' contact with the rest of the country through the media does not always have to be in the English language.

This change in the fortunes of the language is encouraging but the language can survive, in the long term, only if the community achieves a higher level of economic development.

REGIONAL DEVELOPMENT – THE FUTURE

The economic and social problems typical of the Aran Islands today are found, to some extent, on all the offshore islands and western seaboard areas of Ireland. Harsh environmental conditions, small farms and a lack of manufacturing industry have led to continuous emigration which the action of Government agencies has been unable to halt. The EEC has set up a Regional Fund to give a measure of special attention to such "problem regions" in Ireland and other parts of Europe and the Irish Government has offered special inducements to industries in order to attract them to such locations.

But the efforts which have had most success are those which came from within the local community. The people who live in underdeveloped regions are those best acquainted with the nature of their own difficulties and must play a major part in providing solutions. Co-operatives formed on the Aran Islands, for the development of the fishing industry and for the provision of essential services, have achieved significant results in the last ten years. They lack capital however and depend on the State to fund their projects.

The Irish Government is in the process of setting up Údarás na Gaeltachta (The Gaeltacht Authority), an organisation which will concentrate on developing Gaeltacht areas and co-ordinate local effort. The islanders believe that the tide of emigration is now, at long last, beginning to turn, and they look with hope to this new body to help them in their struggle for a secure and prosperous future for their community.

island stories

contents

a day's hunting

maurice o'sullivan

Maurice O'Sullivan was reared on the Blasket Islands off the coast of Co. Kerry. *Fiche Blian ag Fás,* his account of his boyhood on the islands during the period 1910-1920, was translated into English as *Twenty Years A-Growing.* This excerpt describes an expedition by the young Maurice and his friend Tomás, to capture sea birds on the cliffs at the Great Blasket.

THE NEXT DAY, A SUNDAY, was very fine, the sea calm, and not a sound to be heard but the murmur of the waves breaking on the White Strand and the footsteps of men walking down to the quay on their way out to the mainland to Mass.

There were six or seven curraghs out in Mid-Bay by this time, the men in them stripped to their shirts. Soon I saw Tomás coming down.

'God be with you, Tomás.'

'The same God with you. Wouldn't it be a fine day on the hill? Would you have any courage for it?'

'Your soul to the devil, let us go,' said I.

We went up the hill-road together, sweet music in our ears from the heather-hens on the summit. Each of us had a dog.

'Maybe,' said Tomás, 'we would get a dozen of puffins back in the Fern Bottom and another dozen of rabbits. I have a great dog for them.'

We reached Horses' Pound, the heat of the sun cracking the stones and a head of sweat on us. We sat down on a tuft of grass. The devil if Tomás had not a pipe and tobacco. He lit it and handed it to me. 'I don't smoke,' said I. 'Try it,' said he.

When I had had my fill of it, I gave it back to him and stretched myself out on my back in the heat of the sun. But, if so, I soon began to feel Horses' Pound going round me. I was frightened. Tomás was singing to himself.

'Tomás,' said I at last, 'something is coming over me.'

He looked at me. 'It is too much of the pipe you have had. Throw up, and nothing will be on you.'

I would rather have been dead than the way I was, wheezing and whinnying ever and ever till at last I threw up.

When we got to our feet we could not find the dogs. We whistled but they did not come.

'Beauty, Beauty, Beauty,' I cried aloud, for that was the name of my dog.

'Topsy, Topsy, Topsy,' cried Tomás.

At that moment my dog appeared with a rabbit across her mouth. 'My heart for ever, Beauty!' I cried. Then Topsy returned with her mouth empty. 'You can see now which is the better dog,' said I.

We went on to the Fern Bottom and soon my dog had scented a puffin. We began digging the hole but the ground was too firm and we had to give it up. Off with us then as far as White Rocks.

'We have a good chance now for a dozen of rabbits, for the burrows are very shallow here.'

'Look,' said I, 'Beauty has scented something.'

Down we ran. I thrust my hand into the burrow and drew out a fine fat rabbit.

'Your soul to the devil, Topsy has scented another,' shouted Tomás, and away with him down to the hole. Before long we had a dozen and a half.

'We had better take a rest now,' said Tomás, sitting down on the grass. He took out the pipe again and offered it to me. 'Musha, keep it away,' said I; 'I have bought sense from it already.'

It was midday now, the sun in the height of its power and a great heat in it. While we were talking, Tomás rose up on his elbow: 'Do you know where we will go for the rest of the day?'

'Where?'

'Gathering sea-gulls' eggs in the Scórnach.'

Away we went till we reached its mouth. Looking down at the cliff, a feeling of dizziness came over me.

'What mother's son could go down there, Tomás?'

'Arra, man,' said he, with a laugh, 'you only lack practice. I was the same way myself when I came here the first day with Shaun O'Shea. He was for ever urging me till I agreed to go down with him.'

'Maybe you are right. We had better hide the rabbits here on top and not be carrying them down and up again.'

We began to search for a suitable hole.

'There is a good one here, Tomás.'

'The devil, the gulls would find them out there.'

At last we found a place and we did not leave as much as a pinhole without covering it with fern and sods of earth. Then we turned our faces towards the cliff.

Tomás was down before me leaping as light as a goat through the screes, and no wonder, for it is amongst them he had spent his life. 'Take it fine and easy,' he said to me, 'for fear your foot would loosen a stone and hit me on the head as it went down the hill. It is then you would be raising a clamour, Maurice, when you would see me falling over the cliff.'

'Don't be talking that way, Tomás. You make me shiver.'

A cold sweat was coming out on me with the eeriness of the place. I stopped and looked up. When I saw the black rugged cliff standing straight above I began to tremble still more. I looked down and there was nothing below me but the blue depth of the sea: 'God of Virtues!' I cried, 'isn't it a dangerous place I am in!'

I could see Tomás still climbing down like a goat, without a trouble or care in the world. There was a great din in the gully, shining white with the droppings of the sea-birds — kittiwakes, herring-gulls, puffins, guillemots, sea-ravens, razor-bills, black-backed gulls and petrels — each with its own cry and its own nest built in the rock.

I was looking at them and watching them until before long the dizziness left me, while I thought what a hard life they had, foraging for food like any sinner.

As I was thinking, I saw a puffin making straight towards me in from the sea. It was quite near me now, and I saw it had a bundle of sprats across its mouth. It came nearer and nearer until it was only five yards away. It was likely going to land on the rock, I thought, so I lay down in the long heather which was growing around. It came in fearlessly and I made a grab at it with my hand. But it had gone into a burrow beside me. The entrance was covered with bird dung. I began digging it out and it was easy enough, for I had only to thrust my hand back and lift up the ledge of a stone. There was a fine fat whippeen in it. I thrust my hand in to draw it out, but, if so, I wished I had not, for it gave me a savage bite with its beak. When I caught it by the throat it

dug its claws into me so that my hand was streaming with blood
At last I drew it out and killed it.

I arose and looked down. Tomás was nowhere to be seen.

'Tomás,' I cried.

'Tomás,' said the echo, answering me.

'Well,' came up from Tomás far below.

'Well,' repeated the echo, the way you would swear by the
Book there were four of us on the cliff. It seemed to me he was
miles below me. God of Virtues, said I to myself, he will fall
over the cliff as sure as I live. I will go no farther myself anyway.

I was wandering to and fro among the screes until I came across
another burrow with dung at its mouth. Faith, I have another,
said I, taking courage. I began to dig. Soon I had drawn out a fine
fat puffin. At the end of my wanderings I had three dozen.

I was now the happiest hunter on the hills of Kerry. I sat down
on a stone and drew out the bundle of bread I had brought with
me for the day. I ate it hungrily. When I got up and looked at the
whippeens I had thrown in a heap in the hollow beside me, I
wondered how I would carry them home. Then I remembered I
had a rope round my waist. I untied it, took hold of a dozen of
the birds, put their heads together and tied up the dozen in a
single knot. I did the same with the second dozen and the third,
till I had them all on the rope.

The sun was now as round as a plate beyond the Tearacht to
the west, and a path of glittering golden light stretching as far as
the horizon over the sea. I looked down, but Tomás was not
coming yet, for he was a man who never showed haste or hurry so
long as plunder was to be had. I gave a whistle. The echo answered
me as before. Soon after I heard him shouting, 'I am coming!'

Hundreds of birds were flying around, rabbits leaping from one
clump of thrift to another, a fragrant smell from the white heather
and the fern, big vessels far out on the horizon you would think
were on fire in the sunlight, a heat haze here and there in the
ravines, and Kerry diamonds lying all around weakening my eyes
with their sparkle.

Now I could see Tomás climbing slowly up, his face dirty and
smeared with earth and no jersey on him. I laughed aloud when I
saw the look of him. He was climbing from ledge to ledge till he
was within a few yards of me. He had taken off his jersey, tied a
cord round the neck of it and thrown it over his back with
whatever booty he had inside it. Coming up to me he put down
the jersey carefully on the ground.

'The devil take you, Tomás, what have you got?'

'I have guillemots' eggs, razor-bills' eggs and sea-gulls eggs, my boy,' said he, wiping the sweat from his forehead with his cap.

'Your soul to the devil, why didn't you come down, man, and we would have had twice as many?'

'I was too frightened,' said I, pretending I had got no plunder myself. 'I dare say it is as well for us to be starting now.' And going across to my bundle I threw it over my back.

'What have you there?'

'Puffins in plenty.'

'Where did you get them?'

'Here in the scree without stirring out of it.'

'By God, you are the best hunter I ever met.'

We were moving on now up to the head of the cliff. We went on from ledge to ledge and from clump to clump. When we were up at last we lay down to rest.

'Wait till you see the eggs I have,' said Tomás, opening his jersey.

They were a lovely sight, covered with black and red spots. 'We have had a great hunt,' said I.

'Very good indeed. Have you many whippeens?'

'Three dozen.'

'Och, we will never carry them all home. But it is where the trouble will be now if the eggs are not clean after all our pains.'

'Can't you see for yourself they are clean?' said I, laughing.

'Ah, that is not the cleanness I mean; but come with me and we will soon know.'

We went down to the south to a big pool of water in a bog-hole. 'Look now,' said he, taking up an egg, 'if this egg is hatching it will float on the water, but if it is clean it will sink.'

He threw in the egg. It remained floating.

'Och, the devil take it, there is a chick in that one.'

He took it out and broke it against a stone and sure enough there was a chick in it. 'Faith,' said he, 'it is a good beginning.' He put in another in the water and it was the same way again. 'The devil a clean one among them,' said I. 'I am afraid you are right,' said he, throwing in another and not one of them sinking.

He lost heart then after all his walking in the run of the day and all for nothing. Seeing how despondent he was on account of it: 'Don't mind,' said I; 'haven't we enough, each of us with a dozen and a half of rabbits and a dozen and a half of whippeens?'

We divided the spoils, and when we had all done up in bundles we were ready for the journey home. I looked at Tomás again and laughed.

'I don't know in the world why you are laughing at me since morning.'

'Because anyone would think you were an ape you are so dirty.'

'Faith, if I am as dirty as you are, the yellow devil is on me.'

'What would you say to giving ourselves a good dip in the pool?'

'It is a good idea.'

We stripped off all we had and went in, and when we were dressed again we felt so fresh we could have walked the hill twice over.

'The devil, that was a grand dip.'

'Arra, man, I am not the same after it. Now in the name of God let us turn our faces homewards.'

It was growing late. The sun was sinking on the horizon, the dew falling heavily as the air cooled, the dock-leaves closing up for the night, sea-birds crying as they came back to their young, rabbits rushing through the fern as they left their warrens, the sparkle gone out of the Kerry diamonds and a lonesome look coming over the ravines.

'It is night, Tomás.'

'It is. Isn't there a great stretch on the day?'

'There is, and my people will likely be anxious about me for they don't know where I am. They will say it is into some hole I have fallen.'

'Ah, mo léir, it is often I was out and it is only midnight would bring me home.'

'But I am not the same as you.'

'Why not? Amn't I human the same as yourself?'

'Ah, you are an old dog on the hill and your people are used to your being out late and early. It is the first time for me.'

We were now in sight of the village, lamps lit in every house, dogs barking, the houses and rocks clearly reflected in the sea which lay below them without a stir like a well of fresh water, the moon climbing up behind Cnoc a-choma, big and round and as yellow as gold.

We said good-bye and parted, Tomás to his house and I to mine.

mackerel nets

thomas o'flaherty

Thomas O'Flaherty was a native of Inishmore who spent his childhood and part of his adult life on the island. His book *Cliffmen of the West* describes the daily life of the island as he experienced it in the period. "Mackerel Nets", an excerpt from this book, tells of a narrow escape which O'Flaherty had, along with his uncle and two of his cousins, while hauling nets into their curragh.

"IF THE NETS ARE NOT TAKEN when the current is slack with the changing of the tide, they'll never be taken," my uncle said. My father nodded his head towards his crew. My uncle beckoned to me and to my two cousins — sons of an uncle who had died — to come.

I, being the tallest of the four, crawled under the curach, got my shoulders under the first stand. Two men, one on each side of the prow, lifted the boat with me. When I was straight, holding up the prow, another man got under the rear seat and straightened up. A third shouldered a middle seat, and then this boat, that has been likened when carried in this fashion to a "gigantic beetle on stilts", was walked to the water. A fourth member of the crew followed with the oars on his shoulder. Our curach was the first to be laid on the strand ready for launching. We turned her prow to the surf and put the eight oars on the pins. Several men who had not yet decided to go to sea gathered around our curach. We pushed her out until she was afloat. Then the four of us took our seats. We held our oars poised over the water, ready to start rowing at a signal from the look-out man. Six men held the curach straight in the face of the waves while we waited for a lull. Then the look-out shouted hoarsely: "Stick her out! Give her the oars!"

The six men dug their pampootie-clad feet into the sand and pushed the curach quickly towards the sea. Our eight oars struck the water simultaneously. We seemed to be rowing in a pond for a moment, the sea was so smooth. Then the curach rose sharply and almost stood on end, straight as an arrow in a big sea. Down she came on the other side with a crash that set the teeth shaking in our mouths.

As the first sea fell on the strand we rose on another, not as dangerous as the first because we were in deeper water, but bad enough to prove our undoing if the curach's head was turned an inch too far to the right or left.

We rowed, putting our oars far forward and bringing them to a feather with a graceful flourish. My uncle sang joyously in a voice that was everything but melodious. We were now out of danger, in the long lazy swell of the deep water.

As we rowed towards our nets, we could see the prow of another curach rising over the crest of a sea, then disappearing in the trough. Then another curach got safely through the gauntlet of shore breakers.

"The first one is my brother's curach," my uncle said, with a touch of pride. "The one after him is Mícheal Mór O'Dioráin's."

The three most daring skippers leaving Port Murvey were now on the sea, and soon most of the curachs would be out.

We took our markings and shortly we were right over the first pocán. It was attached to the tail end of two pieces of net. Here the water was deep and we had no trouble taking them. The next two pieces were also brought in safely. Now, we must go right up to the edge of the Big Breaker.

"It should be on the point of full tide," my uncle said. "Unless we have them in before the tide turns, we'll have to use the knife on them. This place will be in foam in a few minutes."

We pulled right up to the pocán. One of my cousins took in the buoy, untied it and tossed it to me. I handed it to my uncle, who placed it in the bow with the other two.

Then my cousin stood on the transom and started to haul in the nets. He had a long sharp knife between his teeth. My uncle and I were on our oars. The four oars were on the pins, stretched along the side of the curach, the blades inside. A third man was stowing the nets.

The Big Breaker was between us and Conamara. My uncle kept his steely blue eyes on the giant ridge of water. We had one net aboard and about half the second when he noticed what looked like a puff of smoke on the crest of the breaker.

"Give them the knife!" my uncle shouted to the man on the transom. "Cut, cut, cut! Lay the sticks on her! Every man on the oars!"

Quick as a flash the long, sharp knife fell on the cork rope, severing it in two. The meshes tore with a ripping noise as the curach darted ahead impelled by the sudden, simultaneous stroke of six oars. The foot-rope appeared for a moment on the transom and in the next was severed with one dexterous slash. The knife-man leaped to his seat and now eight oars were bending in a race with the mighty comber that bore down on our stern. It was a race against death.

We turned the curach's head straight towards the strand, the shortest cut in the direction of deep water. The Big Breaker was getting ready to crash all over the shallows. The one following was a forerunner of others, even more dangerous. At the shallowest spot the mighty reef was already white, the moving crest leaving a cloud of spray in its wake.

We strained at the oars, my uncle urging us on. Usually harsh, he was now encouraging us with endearing expressions. We put all our strength into the pull, in such a way that every muscle in the body was in action. We got the last ounce of motion out of every stroke.

"Another minute" — my uncle began. He did not finish the sentence, for at that moment as if by magic the mighty wave suddenly towered at our stern and seemed to be looking down on us, the slightest suggestion of foam on its crest.

"Dead on the oars!" my uncle hissed. "Hold her steady!" Eight oars were dug into the sea as we kept our eyes straight ahead and held the curach's stern straight in the breaker. Would it break on top of us? We did not even look at one another, let alone speak. We sat like stone idols on the thwarts as if we had become suddenly petrified. We were dumb with horror of the monster wave into whose maw we might be sucked any moment.

Suddenly the transom rose until the curach almost stood straight on her prow. Quickly, but in what seemed an eternity to us, the sea swept by, breaking a few yards ahead. For the moment we were safe, unless another one came right after the first. No! We were safe. We bent to our oars again and soon we were in deep water.

We had five of our six nets. The sixth and one anchor would

be lost. Not so bad at all!

By this time the sea was bursting on every shallow in the bay. We lighted our pipes and rowed proudly and contentedly towards the shore.

"We stopped just in time," said the knife-man. "Another moment — "

"If your knife hadn't got the footrope the first slash, 'tis talking to Peter by now we'd be," said my uncle.

the kelp Burners

thomas o'flaherty

In this passage from *Cliffmen of the West*, Thomas O'Flaherty describes a night spent, as a boy, helping the neighbouring men at the kelp kiln.

THEN THERE AROSE INTO THE atmosphere between me and Conamara billows of light smoke floating lazily and vanishing. It was the smoke from a kelp kiln, burning on the White Shore. I longed to see a kelp kiln in action. But I was considered too young to be out at night, and sure there was no fun watching a kelp kiln burning in the daytime! I would ask my mother's permission. She couldn't refuse me anything.

Presently my mother came home with a large can of milk. She noticed my gloomy look and asked me what was the trouble. I did not answer for a while. Then I told her I would like to go to the White Shore where men from Oatquarter were burning kelp. She was silent for a moment.

"They'll be drinking poitín, *a stóir*," she said. "And I don't want you to be around where that cursed stuff is."

"But I have the pledge, mother," I answered.

"That's true, O little son," she said. "Your father would be angry with you, I'm afraid."

"He wouldn't if you gave me leave to go," I urged. She smiled and then she wept and she took me in her arms and kissed me, and for a moment I lost all desire to see the kelp fire — I was so happy. But soon the thirst for adventure overwhelmed me and I looked appealingly at her.

"The teacher wants me to write an essay about kelp-making," I said.

"Put down the kettle and we'll make a cup of tea," she said. "But you mustn't stay late."

It was nearing sunset when I started towards the White Shore. Birds whistled in the ivy clumps on the rocks and in the sally gardens. Cows lowed. Now and then a sheep bleated. Voices of men echoed from the hollow places in the cliffs. I walked jauntily along whistling for myself. For the first time in my life I would be away from home for the night without a guardian. I was getting to be a man!

I was happy to the point of ecstasy. I pictured myself sitting down on a cock of dry seaweed or on a boulder watching the darting flames and the waves of thick black smoke that became lighter as they ascended to the heavens. Perhaps I would have the privilege of helping to carry the weed to the kiln. I would be given tea and bread and treated like a grown-up man. Perhaps I would be praised and that somebody would say: *"Ní ó'n ngréin ná ó'n ngaoith a thógais é* — It is not from the sun or the wind you took it, O son of Michael!"

I had a mile and a half of a walk in front of me.

Every year about the first of May the Big Breaker half way between Aran and Conamara rears its crest and sends mighty waves speeding towards the shore. All along the bayside of the island lesser breakers come in its wake, and the red seaweed that grows on the shallow places is torn up by the roots and carried to land by the currents. The best kelp is made from this red weed if it gets to the shore quickly, and is spread out to dry before it loses some of the precious juice in deep sea holes and in the burrows under the rocks. Seaweed that is washed ashore on a sandy beach is almost useless for kelpmaking.

To the shores of boulders and pebbles the men take their straddled horses, a basket on each side with ropes made of horsehair attached. High over the straddle they pile the seaweed and hold it together with the ropes. And those hard Aran ponies of the Conamara strain pick their way over slippery, moss-covered flags, between large boulders and pebbles that give way under pressure of hoof, with the sureness of goats among the crags of a mountain.

As I stepped along I thought of the work involved in making kelp from the time the first wisp was gathered until the burned seaweed was in the hands of the buyer. Whatever money was made out of kelp was certainly paid for with hard labour.

When the islanders gathered seaweed in the winter and spring to manure their potato gardens they saved the long rods on which the red seaweed grew, laid them on the limestone fences to dry, and then put them in cocks. These rods are rich in iodine.

No seaweed was saved for kelp until the potato gardens were manured. The seaweed that was washed ashore this time of the year was not as good quality as what came in at the end of spring and in the early summer. Furthermore it rained almost continuously during those seasons, making it almost impossible to dry the seaweed. And the potato was the mainstay of the island. As the people would say: *"Cothuíonn sé duine 'gus beithíoch —* It nourishes man and beast."

The seaweed is spread along the roadside or in fields near by the shore. When it is thoroughly dried it is put in cocks until burning time.

When there is a spring tide a long ribbony weed of deep-red colour is cut at low water. It is rated next to red weed in iodine content. Sometimes this seaweed is brought up from the bottom by means of long poles, called *croísiní* because of the wooden blade at the end of the pole which gives it the appearance of a cross. Black weed is also used for kelp-making, but is considered much inferior to the red seaweeds.

The sun was setting in the north-west when I reached the White Shore. It was Michael Donal who was burning, or to give him his full birthday title Michael son of Donal, son of Patrick son of Michael, son of Bartholomew. He was a kinsman of mine so I made bold to ask him if I could help. He smiled and said that he needed a strong man that very minute.

"Do you see that big cock over there" he said. "Well, get a ladder, climb up on it and start tearing the dry fern off the top of it. Don't hurt yourself, son!"

It was an old cock of seaweed that was there since the previous autumn, and it was thatched with fern and heather to protect it from the rain.

Up I went on the cock and I began to tear off the thatch. I broke the straw ropes or *súgáin* with which it was tied. Every now and then I stopped to watch the blazing kiln and the men feeding the devouring fire.

The kiln was young and the men were going light with the seaweed. The coffin-like incinerator was twenty feet long, three feet wide and one and a half feet high. A fire was started with turf, sticks and dry fern. Once the seaweed got to burn with a little breeze, a deluge would not drown it.

I was not long working when Michael's two daughters came with bread and tea. Michael called me.

"Come down here, son, and have the full of your mouth," he said in Gaelic, the modest way an Aran Islander has of inviting you to gorge yourself with food.

Seven of us sat on the shore to eat. The bread was buttered while hot. This was a feast for a bishop. There was enough bread and tea to feed twice the number. Anybody who came around while the meal was being eaten was forced to share in the food. Two men were taking care of the kiln. With a fresh breeze, sprung up out of the northwest, it was burning evenly from end to end.

It was pitch dark now a short distance from the kiln. Like ghosts the two men who were feeding the flames would appear out of the gloom with armfuls of seaweed and vanish again. The two girls who brought the meal sat on boulders in the glare of the light and looked intently at the fire. The men paid no attention to the them, though they were goodlooking girls. Perhaps they were afraid of irascible old Michael. I looked at them and wondered what they were thinking about. Perhaps they were thinking that part of the price of the kelp would pay their way to America. That was the constant thought in those days. As for me, my ambition at that moment was to grow up in Aran, fish, plant potatoes and make kelp. I was in my glory thinking I was doing a man's share of the work.

I listened eagerly to the conversation of the men. They talked of olden times and of the great kilns of kelp they burned, of going to Kilkerrin on the mainland to sell it and the adventures they had. That was the way with Aran Islanders. They had appropriate stories for every season of the year. In the mackerel season they told stories of great hauls of mackerel and the dangers they encountered taking the nets, the prices they got for the fish and their fights with the buyers. It was the same way when they were engaged manuring, planting or digging potatoes, killing rock birds in the high cliffs on the south side of the island, thatching the houses or going down the cliffs for wrack.

About two o'clock the horizon on the north-east lightened and soon crimsoned. The sun was coming up and I was getting sleepy and felt like lying down. Michael advised me to go home and to bed. I told him I would after I saw them rake the kiln. Michael nodded.

"Go light on her now " he ordered. "It's time we gave her the first raking."

Then the men got hold of long iron rods and stripping to the waist they raked the burnt seaweed in the kiln from end to end and from side to side. They shouted to each other to work harder as the sweat poured from their bodies. When the kelp began to run in a molten mass they stopped and threw more seaweed on the kiln.

The kiln would be burned about twelve o'clock the next night. I would be there if I got my mother's consent. I made for home at a steady trot. When I got to the door I lifted the latch noiselessly hoping nobody would hear me come in. But the dog barked a greeting. I sneaked to bed but I was barely inside the clothes when my mother came, put her hand on my forehead and kissed me. Neither of us spoke. I was soon asleep.

spring sowing

liam o'flaherty

IT WAS STILL DARK WHEN MARTIN DELANEY and his wife Mary got up. Martin stood in his shirt by the window a long time looking out, rubbing his eyes and yawning, while Mary raked out the fire coals that had lain hidden in the ashes on the hearth all night. Outside, cocks were crowing and a white streak was rising from the ground, as it were, and beginning to scatter the darkness. It was a February morning, dry, cold and starry.

The couple sat down to their breakfast of tea, bread and butter, in silence. They had only been married the previous autumn and it was hateful leaving a warm bed at such an early hour. They both felt in a bad humour and ate, wrapped in their thoughts. Martin with his brown hair and eyes, his freckled face and his little fair moustache, looked too young to be married, and his wife looked hardly more than a girl, red-cheeked and blue-eyed, her black hair piled at the rear of her head with a large comb gleaming in the middle of the pile, Spanish fashion. They were both dressed in rough homespuns, and both wore the loose white frieze shirt that Inverara peasants use for work in the fields.

They ate in silence, sleepy and bad humoured and yet on fire with excitement, for it was the first day of their first spring sowing as man and wife. And each felt the glamour of that day on which they were to open up the earth together and plant seeds in it. So they sat in silence and bad humour, for somehow the imminence of an event that had been long expected, loved, feared and prepared for, made them dejected. Mary, with her shrewd woman's mind, munched her bread and butter and thought of... Oh, what didn't she think of? Of as many things as there are in life does a woman think in the first joy and anxiety of her mating.

But Martin's mind was fixed on one thought. Would he be able to prove himself a man worthy of being the head of a family by doing his spring sowing well?

In the barn after breakfast, when they were getting the potato seeds and the line for measuring the ground and the spade, a cross word or two passed between them, and when Martin fell over a basket in the half-darkness of the barn, he swore and said that a man would be better off dead than... But before he could finish what he was going to say, Mary had her arms around his waist and her face to his. 'Martin,' she said, 'let us not begin this day cross with one another.' And there was a tremor in her voice. And somehow, as they embraced and Martin kept mumbling in his awkward peasant's voice, 'pulse of my heart, treasure of my life,' and such traditional phrases, all their irritation and sleepiness left them. And they stood there embracing until at last Martin pushed her from him with pretended roughness and said: 'Come, come, girl, it will be sunset before we begin at this rate.'

Still, as they walked silently in their rawhide shoes, through the little hamlet, there was not a soul about. Lights were glimmering in the windows of a few cabins. The sky had a big grey crack in it in the east, as if it were going to burst in order to give birth to the sun. Birds were singing somewhere at a distance. Martin and Mary rested their baskets of seeds on a fence outside the village and Martin whispered to Mary proudly: 'We are first, Mary.' And they both looked back at the little cluster of cabins, that was the centre of their world, with throbbing hearts. For the joy of spring had now taken complete hold of them.

They reached the little field where they were to sow. It was a little triangular patch of ground under an ivy-covered limestone hill. The little field had been manured with seaweed some weeks before, and the weeds had rotted and whitened on the grass. And there was a big red heap of fresh seaweed lying in a corner by the fence to be spread under the seeds as they were laid. Martin, in spite of the cold, threw off everything above his waist except his striped woollen shirt. Then he spat on his hands, seized his spade and cried: 'Now you are going to see what kind of a man you have, Mary.'

'There, now,' said Mary, tying a little shawl closer under her chin. 'Aren't we boastful this early hour of the morning? Maybe I'll wait till sunset to see what kind of a man I have got.'

The work began. Martin measured the ground by the southern fence for the first ridge, a strip of ground four feet wide, and he placed the line along the edge and pegged it at each end. Then he spread fresh seaweed over the strip. Mary filled her apron with seeds and began to lay them in rows, four, three, four. When she was a little distance down the ridge Martin advanced with spade to the head eager to commence.

'Now in the name of God,' he cried, spitting on his palms, 'let us raise the first sod! '

'Oh, Martin, wait till I'm with you!' cried Mary, dropping her seeds on the ridge and running up to him. Her fingers outside her woollen mittens were numb with the cold, and she couldn't wipe them in her apron. Her cheeks seemed to be on fire. She put an arm round Martin's waist and stood looking at the green sod his spade was going to cut, with the excitement of a little child.

'Now for God's sake, girl, keep back! ' said Martin gruffly. 'Suppose anybody saw us trapesing about like this in the field of our spring sowing, what would they take us for but a pair of useless, soft, empty-headed people that would be sure to die of the hunger. Huh! ' He spoke very rapidly, and his eyes were fixed on the ground before him. His eyes had a wild, eager light in them as if some primeval impulse were burning within his brain and driving out every other desire but that of asserting his manhood and of subjugating the earth.

'Oh, what do we care who is looking? ' said Mary; but she drew back at the same time and gazed distantly at the ground. Then Martin cut the sod, and pressing the spade deep into the earth with his foot, he turned up the first sod with a crunching sound as the grass roots were dragged out of the earth. Mary sighed and walked back hurriedly to her seeds with furrowed brows. She picked up her seeds and began to spread them rapidly to drive out the sudden terror that had seized her at that moment when the first sod was turned up and she saw the fierce, hard look in her husband's eyes, that were unconscious of her presence. She became suddenly afraid of that pitiless, cruel earth, the peasant's slave master, that would keep her chained to hard work and poverty all her life until she would sink again into its bosom. Her short-lived love was gone. Henceforth she was only her husband's helper to till the earth. And Martin, absolutely without thought, worked furiously, covering the ridge with black earth, his sharp spade gleaming white as he whirled it sideways to beat the sods.

Then as the sun rose the little valley beneath the ivy-covered hills became dotted with white frieze shirts, and everywhere men worked madly without speaking and women spread seeds. There was no heat in the light of the sun, and there was a sharpness in the still thin air that made the men jump on their spade shafts ferociously and beat the sods as if they were living enemies. Birds hopped silently before the spades, with their heads cocked sideways, watching for worms. Made brave by hunger they often dashed under the spades to secure their food.

Then when the sun reached a certain point all the women went back to the village to get dinner for their men, and the men worked on without stopping. Then the women returned, almost running, each carrying a tin can with a flannel tied around it and a little bundle tied with a white cloth. Martin threw down his spade when Mary arrived back in the field. Smiling at one another they sat under the hill for their meal. It was the same as their breakfast, tea and bread and butter.

'Ah,' said Martin, when he had taken a long draught of tea from his mug, 'is there anything in this world as fine as eating dinner out in the open like this after doing a good morning's work? There, I have done two ridges and a half. That's more than any man in the village could do. Ha! ' And he looked at his wife proudly.

'Yes, isn't it lovely,' said Mary, looking at the black ridges wistfully. She was just munching her bread and butter. The hurried trip to the village and the trouble of getting the tea ready had robbed her of her appetite. She had to keep blowing at the turf fire with the rim of her skirt, and the smoke nearly blinded her. But now, sitting on that grassy knoll, with the valley all round glistening with fresh seaweed and a light smoke rising from the freshly turned earth, a strange joy swept over her. It overpowered that other feeling of dread that had been with her during the morning.

Martin ate heartily, revelling in his great thirst and his great hunger, with every pore of his body open to the pure air. And he looked around at his neighbours' fields boastfully, comparing them with his own. Then he looked at his wife's little round black head and felt very proud of having her as his own. He leaned back on his elbow and took her hand in his. Shyly and in silence, not knowing what to say and ashamed of their gentle feelings, for peasants are always ashamed of feeling refined, they finished eating and still sat hand in hand looking away into the distance. Everywhere the sowers were resting on little knolls, men, women and children sitting in silence. And the great calm of nature in spring filled the atmosphere around them. Everything seemed to sit still and wait until midday had passed. Only the gleaming sun chased westwards at a mighty pace, in and out through white clouds.

Then in a distant field an old man got up, took his spade and began to clean the earth from it with a piece of stone. The rasping noise carried a long way in the silence. That was the signal for a general rising all along the little valley. Young men stretched themselves and yawned. They walked slowly back to their ridges.

Martin's back and his wrists were getting a little sore, and Mary felt that if she stooped again over her seeds that her neck would break, but neither said anything and soon they had forgotten their tiredness in the mechanical movement of their bodies. The strong smell of the upturned earth acted like a drug on their nerves.

In the afternoon, when the sun was strongest, the old men of the village came out to look at their people sowing. Martin's grandfather, almost bent double over his thick stick, stopped in the land outside the field and, groaning loudly, leaned over the fence.

'God bless the work,' he called wheezily.

'And you, grandfather,' replied the couple together, but they did not stop working.

'Ha! ' muttered the old man to himself. 'Ha! He sows well and that woman is good too. They are beginning well.'

It was fifty years since he had begun with his Mary, full of hope and pride, and the merciless soil had hugged them to its bosom ever since, each spring, even by the aged who have spent their lives tilling the earth; so the old man, with his huge red nose and the spotted handkerchief tied around his skull under his black soft felt hat, watched his grandson work and gave him advice.

'Don't cut your sods so long,' he would wheeze, 'you are putting too much soil on your ridge.'

'Ah, woman! Don't plant a seed so near the edge. The stalk will come out sideways.'

And they paid no heed to him.

'Ah,' grumbled the old man, 'In my young days, when men worked from morning till night without tasting food, better work was done. But of course it can't be expected to be the same as it was. The breed is getting weaker. So it is.'

Then he began to cough in his chest and hobbled away to another field where his son Michael was working.

By sundown Martin had five ridges finished. He threw down his spade and stretched himself. All his bones ached and he wanted to lie down and rest. 'It's time to be going home, Mary,' he said.

Mary straightened herself, but she was too tired to reply. She looked at Martin wearily and it seemed to her that it was a great many years since they had set out that morning. Then she thought of the journey home and the trouble of feeding the pigs, putting the fowls into their coops and getting the supper ready and a momentary flash of rebellion against the slavery of being a peasant's wife crossed her mind. It passed in a moment. Martin was saying, as he dressed himself:

'Ha! My soul from the devil, it has been a good day's work. Five ridges done, and each one of them as straight as a steel rod. Begob, Mary it's no boasting to say that ye might well be proud of being the wife of Martin Delaney. And that's not saying the whole of it, my girl. You did your share better than any woman in Inverara could do it this blessed day.'

They stood for a few moments in silence looking at the work they had done. All her dissatisfaction and weariness vanished from Mary's mind with the delicious feeling of comfort that overcame her at having done this work with her husband. They had done it together. They had planted seeds in the earth. The next day and the next day and all their lives, when spring came they would have to bend their backs and do it until their hands and bones got twisted with rheumatism. But night would always bring sleep and forgetfulness.

As they walked home slowly Martin walked in front with another peasant talking about the sowing, and Mary walked behind, with her eyes on the ground, thinking.

Cows were lowing at a distance.

the letter
Liam o'flaherty

IT WAS A SUMMER AFTERNOON. The clear blue sky was dotted with fluttering larks. The wind was still, as if it listened to their gentle singing. From the shining earth a faint smoke arose, like incense, shaken from invisible thuribles in a rhapsody of joy by hosts of unseen spirits. Such peace had fallen on the world! It seemed there was nothing but love and beauty everywhere; fragrant summer air and the laughter of happy birds. Everything listened to the singing larks in brooding thoughtlessness. Yea, even the horned snails lay stretched out on grey stones with their houses on their backs.

There was no loud sound. Nothing asserted its size in a brutal tumult of wind and thunder. Nothing swaggered with a raucous noise to disarrange the perfect harmony. Even the tiny insects mounting the blades of grass with slow feet were giants in themselves and things of pride to nature.

The grass blades, brushing with the movements of their growth, made joyous gentle sounds, like the sighs of a maiden in love.

A peasant and his family were working in a little field beneath the singing larks. The father, the mother and four children were there. They were putting fresh earth around sprouting potato stalks. They were very happy. It was a good thing to work there in the little field beneath the singing larks. Yes. God, maybe, gave music to cheer their simple hearts.

The mother and the second eldest daughter weeded the ridges, passing before the others. The father carefully spread around the stalks the precious clay that the eldest son dug from the rocky bottom of the shallow field. A younger son of twelve years, brought sea sand in a donkey's creels from a far corner of the field. They mixed the sand with the black clay. The fourth child, still almost an infant, staggered about near his mother, plucking weeds slowly and offering them to his mother as gifts.

They worked in silence; except once when by chance the father's shovel slipped on a stone and dislodged a young stalk from its shallow bed. The father uttered a cry. They all looked.

'Oh! Praised be God on high!' the mother said, crossing herself.

In the father's hands was the potato stalk and from its straggling thin roots there hung a cluster of tiny new potatoes, smaller than marbles. Already their seeds had borne fruit and multiplied. They all stood around and wondered. Then suddenly the eldest son, a stripling, spat on his hands and said wistfully:

'Ah! If Mary were here now wouldn't she be glad to see the new potatoes. I remember, on this very spot, she spread seaweed last winter.'

Silence followed this remark. It was of the eldest daughter he had spoken. She had gone to America in early spring. Since then they had only received one letter from her. A neighbour's daughter had written home recently, though, saying that Mary was without work. She had left her first place that a priest had found for her, as a servant in a rich woman's house.

The mother bowed her head and murmured sadly:

'God is good. Maybe to-day we'll get a letter.'

The father stooped again, struck the earth fiercely with his shovel and whispered harshly:

'Get on with the work.'

They moved away. But the eldest son mused for a while looking over the distant hills. Then he said loudly to his mother as if in defiance:

'It's too proud she is to write, mother, until she has money to send. I know Mary. She was always the proud one.'

They all bent over their work and the toddling child began again to bring weeds as gifts to his mother. The mother suddenly caught the child in her arms and kissed him. Then she said:

'Oh! They are like angels singing up there. Angels they are like. Wasn't God good to them to give them voices like that? Maybe if she heard the larks sing she'd write. But sure there are no larks in big cities.'

And nobody replied. But surely the larks no longer sang so happily. Now the sky became immense. The world became immense, an empty dangerous vastness. And the music of the fluttering birds had an eerie lilt to it. So they felt; all except the toddling child, who still came innocently to his mother, bringing little weeds as gifts.

Suddenly the merry cries of children mingled with the triumphant singing of the larks. They all paused and stood erect. Two little girls were running up the lane towards the field. Between the winding fences of the narrow lane they saw the darting white pinafores and the bobbing golden heads of the running girls. Their golden heads flashed in the sunlight. They came running, crying out joyously in trilling girlish voices. They were the two remaining children. They were coming home from school.

'What brought ye to the field?' the mother cried while they were still afar off.

'A letter,' one cried, as she jumped on to the fence of the field.

The father dropped his shovel and coughed. The mother crossed herself. The eldest son struck the ground with his spade and said: 'By the Book!'

'Yes, a letter from Mary,' said the other child, climbing over the fence also and eager to participate equally with her sister in the bringing of the good news. 'The postman gave it to us.'

They brought the letter to their father. All crowded round their father by the fence, where there was a little heap of stones.

The father sat down, rubbed his fingers carefully on his thighs and took the letter. They all knelt around his knees. The mother took the infant in her arms. They all became very silent. Their breathing became loud. The father turned the letter round about in his hands many times, examining it.

'It's her handwriting surely,' he said at length.

'Yes, yes,' said the eldest son. 'Open it, father.'

'In the name of God,' said the mother.

'God send us good news,' the father said, slowly tearing the envelope.

Then he paused again, afraid to look into the envelope. Then one of the girls said:

'Look, look. There's a cheque in it. I see it against the sun.'

'Eh?' said the mother.

With a rapid movement the father drew out the contents of the envelope. A cheque was within the folded letter. Not a word was spoken until he held up the cheque and said:

'Great God, it's for twenty pounds.'

'My darling,' the mother said, raising her eyes to the sky. 'My treasure, I bore you in my womb. My own sweet treasure.'

The children began to laugh, hysterical with joy. The father coughed and said in a low voice:

'There's a horse for that money to be had. A horse.'

'Oh! Father,' said the eldest son. 'A two-year-old and we'll break it on the strand. I'll break it, father. Then we'll have a horse like the people of the village. Isn't Mary great? Didn't I say she was waiting until she had money to send? A real horse!'

'And then I can have the ass for myself, daddy,' said the second boy.

And he yelled with joy.

'Be quiet will ye,' said the mother quietly in a sad tone. 'Isn't there a letter from my darling? Won't ye read me the letter?'

'Here,' said the father. 'Take it and read it one of ye. My hand is shaking.'

It was shaking and there were tears in his eyes, so that he could see nothing but a blur.

'I'll read it,' said the second daughter.

She took the letter, glanced over it from side to side and then suddenly burst into tears.

'What is it?' said the eldest son angrily. 'Give it to me.'

He took the letter, glanced over it and then his face became stern. All their faces became stern.

'Read it, son,' the father said.

' "Dear Parents," ' the son began. ' "Oh, mother, I am so lonely." It's all, all covered with blots same as if she were crying on the paper. "Daddy, why did I .... why did I ever ... ever ..." it's hard to make it out... yes... 'why did I ever come to this awful place? Say a prayer for me every night, mother. Kiss baby for me. Forgive me, mother. Your loving daughter Mary".'

When he finished there was utter silence for a long time. The father was the first to move. He rose slowly, still holding the cheque in his hand. Then he said:

'There was no word about the money in the letter,' he said in a queer voice. 'Why is that now?'

'Twenty pounds,' the mother said in a hollow voice. 'It isn't earned in a week.'

She snatched the letter furtively from her son and hid it ravenously in her bosom.

The father walked away slowly by the fence, whispering to himself in a dry voice:

'Aye! My greed stopped me asking myself that question. Twenty pounds.'

He walked away erect and stiff, like a man angrily drunk.

The others continued to sit about in silence, brooding. They no longer heard the larks. Suddenly one looked up and said in a frightened voice:

'What is father doing?'

They all looked. The father had passed out of the field into another uplying craggy field. He was now standing on a rock with his arms folded and his bare head fallen forward on his chest, perfectly motionless. His back was towards them but they knew he was crying. He had stood that way, apart, the year before, on the day their horse died.

Then the eldest son muttered a curse and jumped to his feet. He stood still with his teeth set and his wild eyes flashing. The infant boy dropped a weed from his tiny hands and burst into frenzied weeping.

Then the mother clutched the child in her arms and cried out in a despairing voice:

'Oh! Birds, birds, why do ye go on singing when my heart is frozen with grief.'

Together they all burst into a loud despairing wail and the harsh sound of their weeping rose into the sky from the field that had suddenly become ugly and lonely; up, up into the clear blue sky where the larks still sang their triumphant melody.

goíng ínto exíle

líam o'flaherty

PATRICK FEENEY'S CABIN WAS CROWDED with people. In the large kitchen men, women and children lined the walls, three deep in places, sitting on forms, chairs, stools, and on one another's knees. On the cement floor three couples were dancing a jig and raising a quantity of dust, which was, however, soon sucked up the chimney by the huge turf fire that blazed on the hearth. The only clear space in the kitchen was the corner to the left of the fireplace, where Pat Mullaney sat on a yellow chair, with his right ankle resting on his left knee, a spotted red handkerchief on his head that reeked with perspiration, and his red face contorting as he played a tattered old accordian. One door was shut and the tins hanging on it gleamed in the firelight. The· opposite door was open and over the heads of the small boys that crowded in it and outside it, peering in at the dancing couples in the kitchen, a starry June sky was visible and, beneath the sky, shadowy grey crags and misty, whitish fields lay motionless, still and sombre. There was a deep, calm silence outside the cabin and within the cabin, in spite of the music and dancing in the kitchen, a starry June sky was visible and beneath the sky, Patrick Feeney's eldest son Michael sat on the bed with three other young men, there was a haunting melancholy in the air.

The people were dancing, laughing and singing with a certain forced and boisterous gaiety that failed to hide from them the real cause of their being there, dancing singing and laughing. For the dance was on account of Patrick Feeney's two children, Mary and Michael, who were going to the United States on the following morning.

Feeney himself, a black-bearded, red-faced, middle-aged

peasant, with white ivory buttons on his blue frieze shirt and his hands stuck in his leather waist belt, wandered restlessly about the kitchen, urging the people to sing and dance, while his mind was in agony all the time, thinking that on the following day he would lose his two eldest children, never to see them again perhaps. He kept talking to everybody about amusing things, shouted at the dancers and behaved in a boisterous and abandoned manner. But every now and then he had to leave the kitchen, under the pretence of going to the pigsty to look at a young pig that was supposed to be ill. He would stand, however, upright against his gable and look gloomily at some star or other, while his mind struggled with vague and peculiar ideas that wandered about in it. He could make nothing at all of his thoughts, but a lump always came up his throat, and he shivered although the night was warm.

Then he would sigh and say with a contraction of his neck: 'Oh, it's a queer world this and no doubt about it. So it is.' Then he would go back to the cabin again and begin to urge on the dance, laughing, shouting and stamping on the floor.

Towards dawn, when the floor was crowded with couples, arranged in fours, stamping on the floor and going to and fro, dancing the 'Walls of Limerick', Feeney was going out to the gable when his son Michael followed him out. The two of them walked side by side about the yard over the grey sea pebbles that had been strewn there the previous day. They walked in silence and yawned without need, pretending to be taking the air. But each of them was very excited. Michael was taller than his father and not so thickly built, but the shabby blue serge suit that he had bought for going to America was too narrow for his broad shoulders and the coat was too wide around the waist. He moved clumsily in it and his hands appeared altogether too bony and big and red, and he didn't know what to do with them. During his twenty-one years of life he had never worn anything other than the home-spun clothes of Inverara, and the shop-made clothes appeared as strange to him and as uncomfortable as a dress suit worn by a man working in a sewer. His face was flushed a bright red and his blue eyes shone with excitement. Now and again he wiped the perspiration from his forehead with the lining of his grey tweed cap.

At last Patrick Feeney reached his usual position at the gable end. He halted, balanced himself on his heels with his hands in his waist belt, coughed and said, 'It's going to be a warm day.' The son came up beside him, folded his arms and leaned his right shoulder against the gable.

'It was kind of Uncle Ned to lend the money for the dance, father,' he said. 'I'd hate to think that we'd have to go without something or other, just the same as everybody else has. I'll send you that money, the very first money I earn, father... even before I pay Aunt Mary for my passage money. I should have all that money paid off in four months, and then I'll have some more money to send you by Christmas.'

And Michael felt very strong and manly recounting what he was going to do when he got to Boston, Massachusetts. He told himself that with his great strength he would earn a great deal of money. Conscious of his youth and his strength and lusting for adventurous life, for the moment he forgot the ache in his heart that the thought of leaving his father inspired in him.

The father was silent for some time. He was looking at the sky with his lower lip hanging, thinking of nothing. At last he sighed as a memory struck him. 'What is it?' said the son. 'Don't weaken, for God's sake. You will only make it hard for me.' 'Fooh! said the father suddenly with pretended gruffness. 'Who is weakening? I'm afraid that your new clothes make you impudent.' Then he was silent for a moment and continued in a low voice: 'I was thinking of that potato field you sowed alone last spring the time I had influenza. I never set eyes on the man that could do it better. It's a cruel world that takes you away from the land that God made you for.'

'Oh, what are you talking about, father?' said Michael irritably. 'Sure what did anybody ever get out of the land but poverty and hard work and potatoes and salt?'

'Ah yes,' said the father with a sigh, 'but it's your own, the land, and over there' — he waved his hand at the western sky — 'you'll be giving your sweat to some other man's land, or what's equal to it.'

'Indeed,' muttered Michael looking at the ground with a melancholy expression in his eyes. 'It's poor encouragement you are giving me.'

They stood in silence fully five minutes. Each hungered to embrace the other, to cry, to beat the air, to scream with excess of sorrow. But they stood silent and sombre, like nature about them, hugging their woe. Then they went back to the cabin. Michael went into the little room to the left of the kitchen, to the three young men who fished in the same curragh with him and were his bosom friends. The father walked into the large bedroom to the right of the kitchen.

The large bedroom was also crowded with people. A large table was laid for tea in the centre of the room and about a dozen young men were sitting at it, drinking tea and eating buttered raisin cake. Mrs. Feeney was bustling about the table, serving the food and urging them to eat. She was assisted by her two younger daughters and by another woman, a relative of her own. Her eldest daughter Mary, who was going to the United States that day, was sitting on the edge of the bed with several other young women. The bed was a large four poster bed with a deal canopy over it, painted red, and the young women were huddled together on it. So that there must have been about a dozen of them there. They were Mary Feeney's particular friends, and they stayed with her in that uncomfortable position just to show how much they liked her. It was a custom.

Mary herself sat on the edge of the bed with her legs dangling. She was a pretty, dark-haired girl of nineteen, with dimpled, plump, red cheeks and ruminative brown eyes that seemed to cause little wrinkles to come and go in her low forehead. Her nose was soft and small and rounded. Her mouth was small and the lips were red and open. Beneath her white blouse that was frilled at the neck and her navy blue skirt that outlined her limbs as she sat on the edge of the bed, her body was plump, soft, well-moulded and in some manner exuded a feeling of freshness and innocence. So that she seemed to have been born to be fondled and admired in luxurious surroundings instead of having been born a peasant's daughter, who had to go to the United States that day to work as a servant or maybe in a factory.

As she sat on the edge of the bed crushing her little handkerchief between her palms, she kept thinking feverishly of the United States, at one moment with fear and loathing, at the next with desire and longing. Unlike her brother she did not think of the work she was going to do or the money that she was going to earn. Other things troubled her, things of which she was half ashamed, half afraid, thoughts of love and of foreign men and of clothes and of houses where there were more than three rooms and where people ate meat every day. She was fond of life, and several young men among the local gentry had admired her in Inverara. But...

She happened to look up and she caught her father's eyes as he stood silently by the window with his hands stuck in his waist belt. His eyes rested on hers for a moment and then he dropped them without smiling, and with his lips compressed he walked down into the kitchen. She shuddered slightly. She was a little afraid of her father, although she knew that he loved her very much and he was very kind to her. But the winter before he had whipped her with a dried willow rod, when he caught her one evening behind Tim Hernon's cabin after nightfall, with Tim Hernon's son Bartly's arms around her waist and he kissing her. Ever since, she always shivered slightly when her father touched her or spoke to her.

'Oho!' said an old peasant who sat at the table with a saucer full of tea in his hand and his grey flannel shirt open at his thin, hairy, wrinkled neck. 'Oho! indeed, but it's a disgrace to the island of Inverara to let such a beautiful woman as your daughter go away, Mrs. Feeney. If I were a young man, I'd be flayed alive if I'd let her go.'

There was a laugh and some of the women on the bed said: 'Bad cess to you, Patsy Coyne, if you haven't too much impudence, it's a caution.' But the laugh soon died. The young men sitting at the table felt embarrassed and kept looking at one another sheepishly, as if each tried to find out if the others were in love with Mary Feeney.

'Oh, well, God is good,' said Mrs. Feeney, as she wiped her lips with the tip of her bright, clean, check apron. 'What will be must be, and sure there is hope from the sea, but there is no hope from the grave. It is sad and the poor have to suffer, but...' Mrs. Feeney stopped suddenly, aware that all these platitudes meant nothing whatsoever. Like her husband she was unable to think intelligently about her two children going away. Whenever the reality of their going away, maybe for ever, three thousand miles into a vast unknown world, came before her mind, it seemed that a thin bar of some hard metal thrust itself forward from her brain and rested behind the wall of her forehead. So that almost immediately she became stupidly conscious of the pain caused by the imaginary bar of metal and she forgot the dread prospect of her children going away. But her mind grappled with the things about her busily and efficiently, with the preparation of food, with the entertaining of her guests, with the numerous little things that have to be done in a house where there is a party and which only a woman can do properly. These little things, in a manner, saved her, for the moment at least, from bursting into tears whenever she looked at her daughter and whenever she thought of her son, whom she loved most of all her children, because perhaps she nearly died giving birth to him and he had been very delicate until he was twelve years old. So she laughed down in her breast a funny laugh she had that made her heave when her check apron rose out from the waist band in a deep curve. 'A person begins to talk,' she said with a shrug of her shoulders sideways, 'and then a person says foolish things.'

'That's true,' said the old peasant, noisily pouring more tea from his cup to his saucer.

But Mary knew by her mother laughing that way that she was very near being hysterical. She always laughed that way before she had one of her fits of hysterics. And Mary's heart stopped beating suddenly and then began again at an awful rate as her eyes became acutely conscious of her mother's body, the rotund, short body with the wonderful mass of fair hair growing grey at the temples and the fair face with the soft liquid brown eyes, that grew hard and piercing for a moment as they looked at a thing and then grew soft and liquid again, and the thin-lipped small mouth with the beautiful white teeth and the deep perpendicular grooves in the upper lip and the tremor that always came in the corner of the mouth, with love, when she looked at the children. Mary became acutely conscious of all these little points, as well as of the little black spot that was on her left breast below the nipple and the swelling that came now and again in her legs and caused her to have hysterics and would one day cause her death. And she was stricken with horror at the thought of leaving her mother and at the selfishness of her thoughts. She had never been prone to thinking of anything important but now, somehow for a moment, she had a glimpse of her mother's life that made her shiver and hate herself as a cruel, heartless, lazy, selfish wretch. Her mother's life loomed up before her eyes, a life of continual misery and suffering, hard work, birth pangs, sickness and again hard work and hunger and anxiety. It loomed up and then it fled again, a little mist came before her eyes and she jumped down from the bed, with the jaunty twirl of her head that was her habit when she set her body in motion.

'Sit down for a while, mother,' she whispered, toying with one of the black ivory buttons on her mother's brown bodice. 'I'll look after the table.' 'No, no,' murmured the mother with a shake of her whole body, 'I'm not a bit tired. Sit down, my treasure. You have a long way to travel to-day.'

And Mary sighed and went back to the bed again.

At last somebody said: 'It's broad daylight.' And immediately everybody looked out and said: 'So it is, and may God be praised.' The change from the starry night to the grey, sharp dawn, was hard to notice until it had arrived. People looked out and saw the morning light sneaking over the crags, silently, along the ground, pushing the mist banks upwards. The stars were growing dim. A long way off invisible sparrows were chirping in their ivied perch in some distant hill or other. Another day had arrived and even as the people looked at it, yawned and began to search for their hats, caps and shawls preparing to go home, the day grew and spread its light and made things move and give voice. Cocks crew, blackbirds carolled, a dog let loose from a cabin by an early riser chased madly after an imaginary robber, barking as if his tail were on fire. The people said goodbye and began to stream forth from Feeney's cabin. They were going to their homes to see to the morning's work before going to Kilmurrage to see the emigrants off on the steamer to the mainland. Soon the cabin was empty except for the family.

All the family gathered into the kitchen and stood about for some minutes talking sleepily of the dance and of the people who had been present. Mrs. Feeney tried to persuade everybody to go to bed, but everybody refused. It was four o'clock and Michael and Mary would have to set out for Kilmurrage at nine. So tea was made and they all sat about for an hour drinking it and eating rasin cake and talking. They only talked of the dance and of the people who had been present.

There were eight of them there, the father and mother and six children. The youngest child was Thomas, a thin boy of twelve, whose lungs made a singing sound every time he breathed. The next was Bridget, a girl of fourteen, with dancing eyes and a habit of shaking her short golden curls every now and then for no apparent reason. Then there were the twins, Julia and Margaret, quiet, rather stupid, flat-faced girls of sixteen. Both their upper front teeth protruded slightly and they were both great workers and very obedient to their mother. They were all sitting at the table, having just finished a third large pot of tea, when suddenly the mother hastily gulped down the remainder of the tea in her cup, dropped the cup with a clatter to her saucer and sobbed once through her nose.

'Now mother,' said Michael sternly, 'what's the good of this work?'

'No, you are right, my pulse,' she replied quietly. 'Only I was just thinking how nice it is to sit here surrounded by all my children, all my little birds in my nest, and then two of them going to fly away made me sad.' And she laughed, pretending to treat it as a foolish joke.

'Oh, that be damned for a story,' said the father, wiping his mouth on his sleeve; 'there's work to be done. You Julia, go and get the horse. Margaret, you milk the cow and see that you give enough milk to the calf this morning.' And he ordered everybody about as if it were an ordinary day of work.

But Michael and Mary had nothing to do and they sat about miserably conscious that they had cut adrift from the routine of their home life. They no longer had any place in it. In a few hours they would be homeless wanderers. Now that they were cut adrift from it, the poverty and sordidness of their home life appeared to them under the aspect of comfort and plenty.

So the morning passed until breakfast time at seven o'clock. The morning's work was finished and the family was gathered together again. The meal passed in a dead silence. Drowsy after the sleepless night and conscious that the parting would come in a few hours, nobody wanted to talk. Everybody had an egg for breakfast in honour of the occasion. Mrs. Feeney, after her usual habit, tried to give her egg first to Michael, then to Mary, and as each refused it, she ate a little herself and gave the remainder to little Thomas who had the singing in his chest. Then the breakfast was cleared away. The father went to put the creels on the mare so as to take the luggage into Kilmurrage. Michael and Mary got the luggage ready and began to get dressed. The mother and the other children tidied up the house. People from the village began to come into the kitchen, as was customary, in order to accompany the emigrants from their home to Kilmurrage.

At last everything was ready. Mrs. Feeney had exhausted all excuses for moving about, engaged on trivial tasks. She had to go into the big bedroom where Mary was putting on her new hat. The mother sat on a chair by the window, her face contorting on account of the flood of tears she was keeping back. Michael moved about the room uneasily, his two hands knotting a big red handkerchief behind his back. Mary twisted about in front of the mirror that hung over the black wooden mantlepiece. She was spending a long time with the hat. It was the first one she had ever worn, but it fitted her beautifully, and it was in excellent taste. It was given to her by the schoolmistress, who was very fond of her, and she herself had taken it in a little. She had an instinct for beauty in dress and deportment.

But the mother, looking at how well her daughter wore the cheap navy blue costume and the white frilled blouse, and the little round black hat with a fat, fluffy, glossy curl covering each ear, and the black silk stockings with blue clocks in them, and the little black shoes that had laces of three colours in them, got suddenly enraged with... She didn't know with what she got enraged. But for the moment she hated her daughter's beauty, and she remembered all the anguish of giving birth to her and nursing her and toiling for her, for no other purpose than to lose her now and let her go away, maybe to be ravished wantonly because of her beauty and her love of gaiety. A cloud of mad jealousy and hatred against this impersonal beauty that she saw in her daughter almost suffocated the mother, and she stretched out her hands in front of her unconsciously and then just as suddenly her anger vanished like a puff of smoke, and she burst into wild tears, wailing: 'My children, oh, my children, far over the sea you will be carried from me, your mother.' And she began to rock herself and she threw her apron over her head.

Immediately the cabin was full of the sound of bitter wailing. A dismal cry rose from the women gathered in the kitchen. 'Far over the sea they will be carried,' began woman after woman, and then they all rocked themselves and hid their heads in their aprons. Michael's mongrel dog began to howl on the hearth. Little Thomas sat down on the hearth beside the dog, and putting his arms around him, he began to cry, although he didn't know exactly why he was crying, but he felt melancholy on account of the dog howling and so many people being about.

In the bedroom the son and daughter, on their knees, clung to their mother, who held their heads between her hands and rained kisses on both heads ravenously. After the first wave of tears she had stopped weeping. The tears still ran down her cheeks, but her eyes gleamed and they were dry. There was a fierce look in them as she searched all over the heads of her two children with them, with her brows contracted, searching with a fierce terror-stricken expression, as if by the intensity of her stare she hoped to keep a living photograph of them before her mind. With her quivering lips she made a queer sound like 'im-m-m-m' and she kept kissing. Her right hand clutched at Mary's left shoulder and with her left she fondled the back of Michael's neck. The two children were sobbing freely. They must have stayed that way a quarter of an hour.

Then the father came into the room, dressed in his best clothes.

He wore a new frieze waistcoat, with a grey and black front and a white back. He held his soft black felt hat in one hand and in the other hand he had a bottle of holy water. He coughed and said in a weak gentle voice that was strange to him, as he touched his son: 'Come now, it is time.'

Mary and Michael got to their feet. The father sprinkled them with holy water and they crossed themselves. Then, without looking at their mother, who lay in the chair with her hands clasped on her lap, looking at the ground in a silent tearless stupor, they left the room. Each hurriedly kissed little Thomas, who was not going to Kilmurrage, and then, hand in hand, they left the house. As Michael was going out the door he picked a piece of loose whitewash from the wall and put it in his pocket. The people filed out after them, down the yard and on to the road, like a funeral procession. The mother was left in the house with little Thomas and two old peasant women from the village. Nobody spoke in the cabin for a long time.

Then the mother rose and came into the kitchen. She looked at the two women, at her little son and at the hearth, as if she were looking for something she had lost. Then she threw her hands into the air and ran out into the yard.

'Come back,' she screamed; 'come back to me.'

She looked wildly down the road with dilated nostrils, her bosom heaving. But there was nobody in sight. Nobody replied. There was a crooked stretch of limestone road, surrounded by grey crags that were scorched by the sun. The road ended in a hill and then dropped out of sight. The hot June day was silent. Listening foolishly for an answering cry, the mother imagined she could hear the crags simmering under the hot rays of the sun. It was something in her head that was singing.

The two old women led her back into the kitchen. 'There is nothing that time will not cure,' said one. 'Yes. Time and patience,' said the other.

the test of courage
liam o'flaherty

AT SUNDOWN on a summer evening Michael O'Hara and Peter Cooke left their village with great secrecy. Crouching behind fences, they made a wide circuit and then ran all the way to a little rock-bound harbour that lay a mile to the southwest. They carried their caps in their hands as they ran and they panted with excitement. They were about to execute a plan of adventure which they had devised for weeks. They were going to take Jimmy the weaver's boat out for a night's bream fishing.

Michael O'Hara was twelve years and four months, five months younger than his comrade. He had very intelligent eyes of a deep-blue colour and his fair hair stood up on end like close-cropped bristles. He looked slender and rather delicate in his blue jersey and grey flannel trousers that only reached half-way down his bare shins. Although it was he who had conceived and planned the adventure, just as he planned all the adventures of the two comrades, he now lagged far behind in the race for the port. This was partly due to his inferior speed. It was also due to a nervous reaction against embarking on an expedition that would cause grave anxiety to his parents.

Peter Cooke looked back after reaching the great mound of boulders that lined the head of the harbour. He frowned and halted when he saw his companion far behind. His sturdy body seemed to be too large for his clothes, which were identical with those worn by O'Hara. His hair was black and curly. His face was freckled. He had the heavy jaws and thick nose of a fighter. His small grey eyes, set close together, lacked the intelligence of Michael O'Hara's eyes.

'Hurry on,' he cried in a loud whisper, when Michael came

closer, 'What ails you? Are you tired already?'

Michael looked back over his shoulder furtively.

'I thought I saw somebody,' he said in a nervous tone.

'Who?' said Peter. 'Who did you see?'

'Over there,' Michael said.

He pointed towards the north in the direction of the village, which was now half hidden by the intervening land. Only the thatched roofs and the smoking chimneys of the houses were visible. The smoke rose straight up from the chimneys in the still twilight. To the west of the village ran a lane, its low fence standing out against the fading horizon of the sky like a curtain full of irregular holes.

'I think it was my mother I saw coming home from milking the cow along the lane,' Michael said in a voice that was slightly regretful. 'I just saw her head over the fence, but it looked like her shawl. I don't think she saw me, though. Even if she did see me, she wouldn't know who it was.'

'Come on,' Peter said. 'She couldn't see you that far away. We have to hurry or it will be dark before we get that curragh in the water.'

As nimbly as goats, the two boys ran down the sloping mound of granite boulders and along the flat stretch of grey limestone that reached out to the limit of the tide. Then they went into a cave beneath a low cliff that bordered the shore. They brought the gear they had hidden in this cave down to the sea's edge and dropped it at the point where they were to launch the boat.

'Do you think we'll be able to carry her down, Peter?' Michael said, as they ran back across the mound of boulders to fetch the boat.

Peter halted suddenly and looked at his comrade. He was irritated by the nervous tone of Michael's voice.

'Are you getting afraid?' he said roughly.

'Who? Me?' said Michael indignantly.

'If you are,' said Peter, 'say the word and we'll go back home. I don't want to go out with you if you start whinging.'

'Who's whinging?' said Michael. 'I only thought we mightn't be able to carry her down to the rock. Is there any harm in that?'

'Come on,' said Peter, 'and stop talking nonsense. Didn't we get under her four times to see could we raise her? We raised her, didn't we? If we could raise her, we can carry her. Jimmy the weaver can rise under her all by himself and he's an old man. He's such a weak old man, too, that no crew in the village would take him out fishing with them. It would be a shame if the two of us weren't as strong as Jimmy the weaver.'

'I hope he won't put a curse on us,' Michael said as they walked along, 'when he finds out that we took his curragh. He's terrible for cursing when he gets angry. I've seen him go on his two knees and curse when two eggs were stolen from under his goose and she hatching. He pulled up his trousers and cursed on his naked knees.'

'He'd be an ungrateful man,' Peter said, 'if he put a curse on us after all we've done for him during the past week. Four times we drew water from the well for him. We dug potatoes for him in his little garden twice and we gave him a rabbit that we caught. The whole village would throw stones at his house if he put a curse on us after we doing all that for him.'

All the village boats usually rested on the flat ground behind the mound of granite boulders. There was a little wall of loose stones around each boat to protect it from the great south winds that sometimes blew in from the ocean. At present only the weaver's boat remained in its stone pen, lying bottom up within its protecting wall, with stone props under the transoms to keep it from the ground. All the other pens were empty, for it was the height of the bream season and the men were at sea.

'Come on now,' Peter said when they reached the boat. 'Lift up the bow.'

They got on each side of the bow and raised it without difficulty.

'You get under it now and settle yourself,' Peter said. Michael crouched and got under the boat, with his face towards the stern. He rested his shoulders against the front seat and braced his elbows against the frame.

Although they had practised raising the boat, he now began to tremble lest he might not be able to bear the weight when Peter raised the stern.

'Keep your legs well apart' Peter said, 'and stand loose same as I told you.'

'I'm ready,' Michael said nervously. 'You go ahead and raise her.'

Peter put on his cap with the peak turned backwards, then he set himself squarely under the stern of the boat. He gritted his teeth and made his strong back rigid. Then he drew in a deep breath and made a sudden effort.

He raised the boat and then spread his legs to distribute the weight. Both boys staggered for a few moments, as they received the full weight of the boat on their shoulders.

'Are you balanced?' Peter said.

'Go ahead,' said Michael.

Peter led the way, advancing slowly with the rhythmic movement of his body which he had copied from his elders. He held his body rigid above the hips, which swayed as he threw his legs forward limply in an outward arc. As each foot touched the ground, he lowered his hips and then raised them again with the shifting of weight to the other foot.

Michael tried to imitate this movement, but he was unable to do it well owing to his nervousness. In practice he had been just as good as Peter. Now, however, the memory of his mother's shawled head kept coming into his mind to disturb him.

'Try to keep in step,' Peter called out, 'and don't grip the frame. Let your shoulders go dead.'

'I'm doing my best,' Michael said, 'but it keeps shifting on my shoulders.'

'That's because you're taking a grip with your hands. Let your shoulders go dead.'

They were both exhausted when they finally laid down the boat on the weed-covered rock by the sea's edge. They had to rest a little while. Then they gently pushed the boat into the water over the smooth carpet of red weed. They had to do this very carefully, because the coracle was just a light frame of thin pine lathes covered with tarred canvas. The least contact with a sliver of stone or even with a limpet cone, could have put a hole in the canvas. Fortunately the sea was dead calm, and they managed the launching without accident.

'Now, in God's name,' Peter said, imitating a man's voice as he dipped his hand in the seawater and made the sign of the Cross on his forehead according to ritual, 'I'll go aboard and put her under way. You hand in the gear when I bring her stern to shore.'

He got into the prow seat, unshipped the oars and dipped the glambs in the water before fixing them on the thole pins. Then he manoeuvred the stern of the boat face to the rock. Michael threw aboard the gear, which included a can of half-baited limpets for bait, four lines coiled on small wooden frames, half a loaf of bread rolled up in a piece of cloth, and the anchor rope with a large granite stone attached. Then he also dipped his right hand in the brine water and made the sign of the Cross on his forehead.

'In God's name,' he said reverently, as he put one knee on the stern and pushed against the rock with his foot, 'head her out.'

As Peter began to row, Michael took his seat on the after transom and unshipped his oars. He dipped the glambs in the water and put the oars on the thole pins.

'Face land, right hand underneath,' Peter called out just like a grown-up captain giving orders to his crew.

'I'm with you,' Michael said. 'Head her out.'

The two boys rowed well, keeping time perfectly. Soon they had cleared the mouth of the little harbour and they were in the open sea. Night was falling, but they could see the dark cluster of village boats beneath a high cliff to the west. They turned east.

'Take a mark now and keep her straight,' Peter said.

Michael brought two points on the dim land to the west into line with the stern and they rowed eastwards until they came abreast of a great pile of rock that had fallen from the cliff. Here they cast anchor. When they had tied the anchor rope to the cross-stick in the bow, the boat swung round and became motion-less on the still water.

'Oh!, You devil!' Peter said excitedly. 'Out with the lines now and let us fish. Wouldn't it be wonderful if we caught a boat load of bream. We'd be the talk of the whole parish.'

'Maybe we will,' cried Michael, equally excited.

Now he was undisturbed by the memory of his mother's shawled head. Nor was he nervous about his position, out at night on a treacherous ocean in a frail coracle. The wild rapture of adventure had taken full possession of him.

Such was the haste with which they baited and paid out their lines that they almost transfixed their hands with the hooks. Each boy paid out two lines, one on either side of the boat. They had cast anchor right in the midst of a school of bream. Peter was the first to get his lines into water. They had barely sunk when he got a strike on both of them.

'Oh! You devil! he cried. 'I've got two.'

In his excitement he tried to haul the two lines simultaneously and lost both of the soft-lipped fish. In the meantime, Michael also got a strike on one of his lines. He swallowed his breath and hauled rapidly. A second fish struck while he was hauling the first line. He also became greedy and grabbed the second line letting the first fish escape. But he landed the second fish.

'Oh! Peter, he cried, 'we'll fill the boat like you said.'

He put the fish smartly between his knees and pulled the hook from its mouth. He dropped it on the bottom of the boat, where it began to beat a tattoo with its tail.

'Oh! You Devil! Peter cried. 'The sea is full of them.'

He had again thrown his lines into the water and two fish immediately impaled themselves on the hooks. This time he landed both fish, as the lessening of excitement enabled him to use his skill.

'We should have brought more limpets,' Michael said, 'This lot we brought won't be half enough!'

The fish continued to strike. Despite losing a large percentage, they had caught thirty-five before an accident drove the boat away from the school. A light breeze had come up from the land. It hardly made a ripple on the surface of the sea, yet its impact caused the boat to lean away from the restraint of the anchor rope. The rope went taught. Then the anchor stone slipped from the edge of a reef on which it had dropped. Falling into deeper water, it could not find ground. The boat swung round and began to drift straight out to sea, pressed by the gentle breeze. The two boys, intent on their fishing, did not notice the accident. Soon, however, the fish ceased to strike. They did not follow the boat into deep water. The lines hung idly over the sides.

'They're gone, Michael said. 'Do you think it's time for us to go home?'

'We can't go home yet,' Peter said indignantly. 'We have only thirty-five fish yet. Wait until they begin to strike again when the tide turns. Then you'll see that we'll fill the boat. In any case, we can't go back until the moon rises. It's too dark now to make our way past the reef.'

'It's dark all right,' Michael said in a low voice. 'I can't see land, though it's so near.'

Now that the fish had gone away, the vision of his mother's shawled head returned to prick his conscience, and the darkness frightened him as it always did. Yet he dared not insist on trying to make port, lest Peter might think he was a coward.

'They'll start biting again, Peter continued eagerly. 'You wait and see. We'll fill the boat. Then the moon will be up and it will be lovely rowing into port. Won't they be surprised when they see all the fish we have? They won't say a word to us when we bring home that awful lot of fish.

Michael shuddered on being reminded of the meeting with his parents after his escapade.

'I'm hungry,' he said. 'Do you think we should eat our bread?

No use bringing it back home again.'

'I'm hungry, too,' Peter said. 'Let's eat the bread while we're waiting for the tide to turn.'

They divided the half loaf and began to eat ravenously. When they had finished, Michael felt cold and sleepy.

'We should have brought more clothes to put on us,' he said. 'The sea gets awful cold at night, doesn't it?'

'Let's lie up in the bow,' Peter said, 'I feel cold myself. We'll lie together in the shelter of the bow while we're waiting for the tide to turn. That way we won't feel the cold in the shelter of the bow.'

They lay down in the bow side by side. There was just room enough for their two bodies stretched close together.

'It's much warmer this way sure enough,' Michael said sleepily.

'It's just like being in bed,' Peter said, 'Oh! You Devil! When I grow up I'll be a sailor. Then I can sleep every night out in the middle of the sea.'

They fell asleep almost at once. In their sleep they put their arms about one another. The moon rose and its eerie light fell on them, as they lay asleep in the narrow bow rocked gently by the boat's movement, to the soft music of the lapping water. The moonlight fell on the dark sides of the boat that drifted before the breeze. It shone on the drifting lines that hung from the black sides, like the tentacles of an evil monster that was carrying the sleeping boys out far over the empty ocean.

The dead fish were covered with a phosphorescent glow when the boat swayed towards the moon.

Then the moonlight faded and dawn came over the sea. The sun rose in the east and its rays began to dance on the black canvas. Michael was the first to awaken. He uttered a cry of fright when he looked about him and discovered where he was. The land was now a great distance. It was little more than a dot on the far horizon. He gripped Peter by the head with both hands.

'Wake up, Peter, he cried. 'Oh! Wake up. Something terrible has happened.'

Thinking he was at home in bed, Peter tried to push Michael away and to turn over on his other side.

'It's not time to get up yet,' he muttered.

When he finally was roused and realized what had happened, he was much more frightened than Michael.

'Oh! You Devil!' he said. 'we pulled anchor. We're lost.'

There was a look of ignorant panic in his small eyes. Michael bit his lip, in an effort to keep himself from crying out loud. It was a great shock to find that Peter, who had always been the leader of the two comrades and who had never before shown any signs of fear, was now in panic.

'We're not lost,' he said angrily. 'Will you look where the land is?' cried Peter. 'Will you look?'

Suddenly Michael felt that he no longer wanted to cry. His eyes got a hard and almost cruel expression in them.

'Stand up, will you?' he said sharply. 'Let me pull the rope.'

Peter looked at Michael stupidly and got out of the way. He sat on the forward transom, while Michael hauled in the anchor rope.

'What could we do?' he said. 'We're lost unless they come and find us. We could never row that far with the wind against us.'

'Why don't you give me a hand with the rope and stop whinging?' cried Michael angrily.

Peter was roused by this insult from a boy whom he had until now been able to dominate. He glared at Michael, spat on his hands and jumped to his feet.

'Get out of my way,' he said gruffly. 'Give me a hold of that rope. Look who's talking about whinging.'

With his superior strength, Peter quickly got the rope and anchor stone into the bow. Then the two of them hauled in the lines. They did not trouble to wind them on the frames but left them lying in a tangled heap on the bottom.

'Hurry up' Peter kept saying. 'We have to hurry out of here.' Still roused to anger by Michael's insult, he got out his oars and turned the bow towards the dot of land on the horizon. Michael also got out his oars.

'Left hand on top,' Peter shouted, 'and give it your strength. Stretch to it. Stretch.'

'We better take it easy,' Michael said. 'We have a long way to go.'

'Stretch to it, I tell you,' Peter shouted still more loudly. 'Give it your strength if you have any.'

As soon as he found the oars in his hands, as a means of escape from what he feared, he allowed himself again to go into a panic. He rowed wildly, leaping from the transom with each stroke.

'Why can't you keep time?' Michael shouted at him.

'Keep time with the stern. You'll only kill yourself that way.'

'Row you devil and stop talking,' cried Peter. 'Give length to your stroke and you'll be able to row with me.'

'But you're supposed to keep with me' Michael said. 'You're supposed to keep with the stern.'

Suddenly Peter pulled so hard that he fell right back off the transom of the bow. One of the oars jumped off the thole pin as he fell backwards. It dropped over the side of the boat and began to drift astern. Michael turned the boat and picked up the oar.

'Don't do that again, he said as he gave the oar to Peter. 'Listen to what I tell you and row quietly.'

Peter looked in astonishment at the cruel eyes of his comrade. He was now completely dominated by them.

'It's no use, Michael,' he said dejectedly. 'You see the land is as far away as ever. It's no use trying to row.'

'We'll make headway if we row quietly,' Michael said. 'Come on now. Keep time with the stern.'

Now that he had surrendered to the will of his comrade Peter rowed obediently in time with the stern oars. The boat began to make good way.

'That's better,' Michael said, when they had been rowing a little while. 'They'll soon be out looking for us,' said Peter. 'Sure nobody saw us leave the port'.

'They'll see the boat is gone,' Michael said. 'Why can't you have sense? I bet they're out looking for us now. All we have to do is to keep rowing quietly.'

'And how would they see us?' Peter said after a pause. 'We can hardly see that land from here, even though it's so big. How could they see this curragh from the land and it no bigger than a thimble on the water?'

Michael suddenly raised his voice and said angrily: 'Is it how you want us to lie down and let her drift away until we die of hunger and thirst? Stop talking and row quietly. You'll only tire yourself out with your talk.'

'Don't you be shouting at me, Michael O'Hara.' Peter cried. 'You better watch out for yourself. Is it how you think I'm afraid of you?'

They rowed in silence after that for more than two hours. The boat made good way and the land became much more distinct on the horizon. It kept rising up from the ocean and assuming its normal shape. Then Peter dropped his oars and let his head hang forward on his chest. Michael went forward to him.

'I'm thirsty' Peter said. 'I'm dying with the thirst. Is there any sign of anybody coming?'

'There is no sign yet, Peter,' Michael said gently. 'We have to have courage, though. They'll come all right. Let you lie down in the bow for a while. I'll put your jersey over your face to keep the sun from touching you. That way you won't feel the thirst so much, I heard my father say so.'

He had to help Peter into the bow, as the older boy was completely helpless with exhaustion. He pulled off Peter's jersey and put it over his face.

'Lie there for a while' he said, 'and I'll keep her from drifting. Then you can spell me.'

He returned to his seat and continued to row. He suffered terribly from thirst. He was also beginning to feel the first pangs of sea-hunger. Yet he experienced an exaltation that made him impervious to this torture. Ever since his imagination had begun to develop, he had been plagued by the fear that he would not be able to meet danger with courage. Even though he deliberately sought out little dangers and tested himself against them without flinching, he continued to believe that the nervousness he felt on these occasions was a sign of cowardice and that he would fail when the big test came.

Now that the big test had come, he experienced the first dark rapture of manhood instead of fear. His blue eyes were no longer soft and dreamy. They had a look of sombre cruelty in them, the calm arrogance of the fighting male. His mind was at peace, because he was now free from the enemy that had lurked within him. Even the pain in his bowels and in his parched throat only served to excite the triumphant will of his awakening manhood. When his tired muscles could hardly clutch the oars within his blistered palms, he still continued to row mechanically.

In the afternoon, when the village boats finally came to the rescue, Michael was still sitting on his transom, trying to row feebly. By then he was so exhausted that he did not hear the approach of the boats until a man shouted from the nearest one of them. Hearing the shout he fell from his seat in a faint.

When he recovered consciousness, he was in the bow of his father's boat. His father was holding a bottle of water to his lips. He looked up into his father's rugged face and smiled when he saw there was no anger in it. On the contrary, he had never before seen such tenderness in his father's stern eyes.

'Was it how you dragged anchor?' his father said.

Although his upper lip was twitching with emotion, he spoke in a casual tone, as to a comrade.

'It could happen to the best of men,' the father continued

thoughtfully after Michael had nodded his head. 'There's no harm done though, thank God.'

He put some clothes under the boy's head, caressed him roughly and told him to go to sleep. Michael closed his eyes. In another boat, Peter's father was shouting in an angry tone.

Michael opened his eyes again when his father and the other men in the boat had begun to row. He looked at the muscular back of his father, who was rowing in the bow seat. A wave of ardent love for his father swept through his blood, making him feel tender and weak. Tears began to stream from his eyes, but they were tears of joy because his father had looked at him with tenderness and spoken to him as to a comrade.

RÍOERS to the sea

J.m. synge

PERSONS IN THE PLAY

MAURYA, *an old woman*
BARTLEY, *her son*

CATHLEEN, *her daughter*
NORA, *a younger daughter*
MEN AND WOMEN

SCENE – *An island off the West of Ireland*

Cottage kitchen, with nets, oilskins, spinning-wheel, some new boards standing by the wall, etc. Cathleen, a girl of about twenty finishes kneading cake, and puts it down in the pot-oven by the fire; then wipes her hands, and begins to spin at the wheel. Nora, a young girl, puts her head in at the door.

Nora *(in a low voice).* Where is she?

Cathleen. She's lying down, God help her, and maybe sleeping, if she's able.

Nora *comes in softly, and takes a bundle from under her shawl.*

Cathleen *(spinning the wheel rapidly).* What is it you have?

Nora. The young priest is after bringing them. It's a shirt and a plain stocking were got off a drowned man in Donegal.

Cathleen *stops her wheel with a sudden movement, and leans out to listen.*

Nora We're to find out if it's Michael's they are, some time herself will be down looking by the sea.

Cathleen. How would they be Michael's, Nora? How would he go to the length of that way to the far north?

Nora. The young priest says he's known the like of it.

'If it's Michael's they are,' says he, 'you can tell herself he's got a clean burial, by the grace of God; and if they're not his, let no one say a word about them, for she'll be getting her death,' says he, 'with crying and lamenting.'

The door which Nora half closed is blown open by a gust of wind.

Cathleen *(looking out anxiously).* Did you ask him would he stop Bartley going this day with the horses to the Galway fair?

Nora. 'I won't stop him,' says he; 'but let you not be afraid. Herself does be saying prayers half through the night, and the Almighty God won't leave her destitute,' says he, 'with no son living.'

Cathleen. Is the sea bad by the white rocks, Nora?

Nora. Middling bad, God help us. There's a great roaring in the west, and it's worse it'll be getting when the tide's turned to the wind. *(She goes over to the table with the bundle).* Shall I open it now?

Cathleen. Maybe she'd wake up on us and come in before we'd done*(Coming to the table).* It's a long time we'll be, and the two of us crying.

Nora *(goes to the inner door and listens).* She's moving about on the bed. She'll be coming in a minute.

Cathleen. Give me the ladder, and I'll put them up in the turf-loft, the way she won't know of them at all, and maybe when the tide turns she'll be going down to see would he be floating from the east.

They put the ladder against the gable of the chimney.

Cathleen *goes up a few steps and hides the bundle in the turf-loft.* Maurya *comes from the inner room.*

Maurya *(looking up at* Cathleen *and speaking querulously).* Isn't it turf enough you have for this day and evening?

Cathleen. There's a cake baking at the fire for a short space *(throwing down the turf),* and Bartley will want it when the tide turns if he goes to Connemara.

Nora *picks up the turf and puts it round the pot-oven.*

Maurya *(sitting down on a stool at the fire).* He won't go this day with the wind rising from the south and west. He won't go this day, for the young priest will stop him surely.

Nora. He'll not stop him, mother; and I heard Eamon Simon and Stephen Pheety and Colum Shawn saying he would go.

Maurya. Where is he itself?

Nora. He went down to see would there be another boat sailing in the week, and I'm thinking it won't be long till he's here now, for the tide's turning at the green head, and the hooker's tacking from the east.

Cathleen. I hear some one passing the big stones.

Nora *(looking out).* He's coming now, and he in a hurry.

Bartley *(comes in and looks round the room. Speaking sadly and quietly).* Where is the bit of new rope, Cathleen, was bought in Connemara?

Cathleen *(coming down)*. Give it to him, Nora; it's on a nail by the white boards. I hung it up this morning, for the pig with the black feet was eating it.

Nora *(giving him a rope)*. Is that it, Bartley?

Maurya. You'd do right to leave that rope, Bartley, hanging by the boards. (Bartley *takes the rope*). It will be wanting in this place, I'm telling you, if Michael is washed up tomorrow morning or the next morning, or any morning in the week; for it's a deep grave we'll make him, by the grace of God.

Bartley *(beginning to work with the rope)*. I've no halter the way I can ride down on the mare, and I must go now quickly. This is the one boat going for two weeks or beyond it, and the fair will be a good fair for horses, I heard them saying below.

Maurya. It's a hard thing they'll be saying below if the body is washed up and there's no man in it to make the coffin, and I after giving a big price for the finest white boards you'd find in Connemara.

She looks round at the boards.

Bartley. How would it be washed up, and we after looking each day for nine days, and a strong wind blowing a while back from the west and south?

Maurya. If it isn't found itself, that wind is raising the sea, and there was a star up against the moon, and it is rising in the night. If it was a hundred horses, or a thousand horses, you had itself, what is the price of a thousand horses against a son where there is one son only?

Bartley *(working at the halter, to* Cathleen). Let you go down each day, and see the sheep aren't jumping in on the rye, and if the jobber comes you can sell the pig with the black feet if there is a good price going.'

Maurya. How would the like of her get a good price for a pig?

Bartley *(to* Cathleen*)*. If the west wind holds with the last bit of the moon let you and Nora get up weed enough for another cock for the kelp. It's hard set we'll be from this day with no one in it but one man to work.

Maurya. It's hard set we'll be surely the day you're drowned with the rest. What way will I live and the girls with me, and I an old woman looking for the grave?

Bartley *lays down the halter, takes off his old coat, and puts on a newer one of the same flannel.*

Bartley *(to* Nora*)*. Is she coming to the pier?

Nora *(looking out)* She's passing the green head and letting fall her sails.

Bartley *(getting his purse and tobacco)*. I'll have half an hour to go down, and you'll see me coming again in two days, or in three days, or maybe in four days if the wind is bad.

Maurya *(turning round to the fire, and putting her shawl over her head)*. Isn't it a hard and cruel man won't hear a word from an old woman, and she holding him from the sea?

Cathleen. It's the life of a young man to be going on the sea, and who would listen to an old woman with one thing and she saying it over?

Bartley *(taking the halter)*. I must go now quickly. I'll ride down on the red mare, and the grey pony'll run behind me.... The blessing of God on you.

He goes out.

Maurya *(crying out as he is in the door)*. He's gone now, God spare us, and we'll not see him again. He's gone now, and when the black night is falling I'll have no son left me in the world.

Cathleen. Why wouldn't you give him your blessing and he looking round in the door? Isn't it sorrow enough is on every one in this house without you sending him out with an unlucky word behind him, and a hard word in his ear?

Maurya *takes up the tongs and begins raking the fire aimlessly without looking round.*

Nora *(turning towards her)*. You're taking away the turf from the cake.

Cathleen *(crying out)*. The Son of God forgive us, Nora, we're after forgetting his bit of bread. *(She comes over to the fire)*.

Nora. And it's destroyed he'll be going till dark night, and he after eating nothing since the sun went up.

Cathleen *(turning the cake out of the oven)*. It's destroyed he'll be, surely. There's no sense left on any person in a house where an old woman will be talking for ever.

Maurya *sways herself on her stool.*

Cathleen *(cutting off some of the bread and rolling it in a cloth; to* Maurya*)*. Let you go down now to the spring well and give him this and he passing. You'll see him then and the dark word will be broken, and you can say 'God speed you,' the way he'll be easy in his mind.

Maurya *(taking the bread).* Will I be in it as soon as himself?

Cathleen. If you go now quickly.

Maurya *(standing up unsteadily).* It's hard set I am to walk.

Cathleen *(looking at her anxiously).* Give her the stick, Nora, or maybe she'll slip on the big stones.

Nora. What stick?

Cathleen. The stick Michael brought from Connemara.

Maurya *(taking a stick* Nora *gives her).* In the big world the old people do be leaving things after them for their sons and children, but in this place it is the young men do be leaving things behind for them that do be old.

She goes out slowly. Nora *goes over to the ladder.*

Cathleen. Wait, Nora, maybe she'd turn back quickly. She's that sorry, God help her, you wouldn't know the thing she'd do.

Nora. Is she gone round by the bush?

Cathleen *(looking out).* She's gone now. Throw it down quickly, for the Lord knows when she'll be out of it again.

Nora *(getting the bundle from the loft).* The young priest said he'd be passing tomorrow, and we might go down and speak to him below if it's Michael's they are surely.

Cathleen *(taking the bundle).* Did he say what way they were found?

Nora *(coming down).* 'There were two men,' says he, 'and they rowing round with poteen before the cocks crowed, and the oar of one of them caught the body, and they passing the black cliffs of the north.'

Cathleen *(trying to open the bundle).* Give me a knife, Nora; the string's perished with the salt water, and there's a black knot on it you wouldn't loosen in a week.

Nora *(giving her a knife).* I've heard tell it was a long way to Donegal.

Cathleen *(cutting the string).* It is surely. There was a man in here a while ago – the man sold us that knife – and he said if you set off walking from the rocks beyond, it would be in seven days you'd be in Donegal.

Nora. And what time would a man take, and he floating?

Cathleen *opens the bundle and takes out a bit of a shirt and a stocking. They look at them eagerly.*

Cathleen *(in a low voice).* The Lord spare us, Nora! isn't it a queer hard thing to say if it's his they are surely?

Nora. I'll get his shirt off the hook the way we can put the one flannel on the other. *(She looks through some clothes hanging* *in the corner).* It's not with them, Cathleen, and where will it be?

Cathleen. I'm thinking Bartley put it on him in the morning, for his own shirt was heavy with the salt in it. *(Pointing to the corner).* There's a bit of a sleeve was of the same stuff. Give me that and it will do.

Nora *brings it to her and they compare the flannel.*

Cathleen. It's the same stuff, Nora; but if it is itself, aren't there great rolls of it in the shops of Galway, and isn't it many another man may have a shirt of it as well as Michael himself?

Nora *(who has taken up the stocking and counted the stitches, crying out).* It's Michael, Cathleen, it's Michael; God spare his soul, and what will herself say when she hears this story, and Bartley on the sea?

Cathleen *(taking the stocking).* It's a plain stocking.

Nora. It's the second one of the third pair I knitted, and I put up three-score stitches, and I dropped four of them.

Cathleen *(counts the stitches).* It's that number is in it *(crying out).* Ah, Nora, isn't it a bitter thing to think of him floating that way to the far north, and no one to keen him but the black hags that do be flying on the sea?

Nora *(swinging herself half round, and throwing out her arms on the clothes).* And isn't it a pitiful thing when there is nothing left of a man who was a great rower and fisher but a bit of an old shirt and a plain stocking?

Cathleen *(after an instant).* Tell me is herself coming, Nora? I hear a little sound on the path.

Nora *(looking out).* She is, Cathleen. She's coming up to the door.

Cathleen. Put these things away before she'll come in. Maybe it's easier she'll be after giving her blessing to Bartley, and we won't let on we've heard anything the time he's on the sea.

Nora *(helping* Cathleen *to close the bundle).* We'll put them here in the corner.

They put them into a hole in the chimney corner. Cathleen *goes back to the spinning-wheel.*

Nora. Will she see it was crying I was?

Cathleen. Keep your back to the door the way the light'll not be on you.

Nora *sits down at the chimney corner, with her back to the door.* Maurya *comes in very slowly, without looking at the girls, and goes over to her stool at the other side of the fire. The cloth with the bread is still in her hand. The girls look at each other, and*

Nora *points to the bundle of bread.*

Cathleen *(after spinning for a moment).* You didn't give him his bit of bread?

Maurya *begins to keen softly, without turning round.*

Cathleen. Did you see him riding down?

Maurya *goes on keening.*

Cathleen *(a little impatiently).* God forgive you; isn't it a better thing to raise your voice and tell what you seen, than be making lamentation for a thing that's done? Did you see Bartley, I'm saying to you?

Maurya *(with a weak voice).* My heart's broken from this day.

Cathleen *(as before).* Did you see Bartley?

Maurya. I seen the fearfulest thing.

Cathleen *(leaves her wheel and looks out).*   God forgive you; he's riding the mare now over the green head, and the grey pony behind him.

Maurya *(starts, so that her shawl falls back from her head and shows her white tossed hair. With a frightened voice).* The grey pony behind him...

Cathleen *(coming to the fire).* What is it ails you at all?

Maurya *(speaking very slowly).* I've seen the fearfulest thing any person has seen since the day Bride Dara seen the dead man with the child in his arms.

Cathleen *and* **Nora.** Uah.

They crouch down in front of the old woman at the fire.

Nora. Tell us what it is you seen.

Maurya. I went down to the spring well, and I stood there saying a prayer to myself. Then Bartley came along, and he riding on the red mare with the grey pony behind him *(she puts up her hands, as if to hide something from her eyes).* The Son of God spare us, Nora!

Cathleen. What is it you seen?

Maurya. I seen Michael himself.

Cathleen *(speaking softly).* You did not, mother. It wasn't Michael you seen, for his body is after being found in the far north, and he's got a clean burial, by the grace of God.

Maurya *(a little defiantly).* I'm after seeing him this day, and he riding and galloping. Bartley came first on the red mare, and I tried to say 'God speed you,' but something choked the words in my throat. He went by quickly; and 'the blessing of God on you,' says he, and I could say nothing. I looked up then, and I crying, at the grey pony, and there was Michael upon it – with fine clothes on him, and new shoes on his feet.

Cathleen *(begins to keen).* It's destroyed we are from this day. It's destroyed, surely.

Nora. Didn't the young priest say the Almighty God won't leave her destitute with no son living?

Maurya *(in a low voice, but clearly).* It's little the like of him knows of the sea... Bartley will be lost now, and let you call in Eamon and make me a good coffin out of the white boards, for I won't live after them. I've had a husband, and a husband's father. and six sons in this house — six fine men, though it was a hard birth I had with every one of them and they coming into the world — and some of them were found and some of them were not found, but they're gone now the lot of them... There was Stephen and Shawn were lost in the great wind, and found after in the Bay of Gregory of the Golden Mouth, and carried up the two of them on one plank, and in by that door.

She pauses for a moment, the girls start as if they heard some-thing through the door that is half open behind them.

Nora *(in a whisper).* Did you hear that, Cathleen? Did you hear a noise in the north-east?

Cathleen *(in a whisper).* There's someone after crying out by the seashore.

Maurya *(continues without hearing anything).* There was Sheamus and his father, and his own father again, were lost in a dark night, and not a stick or sign was seen of them when the sun went up. There was Patch after was drowned out of a curagh that turned over. I was sitting here with Bartley, and he a baby lying on my two knees, and I seen two women, and three women, and four women coming in, and they crossing themselves and not saying a word. I looked out then, and there were men coming after them, and they holding a thing in the half of a red sail, and water dripping out of it — it was a dry day, Nora — and leaving a track to the door.

She pauses again with her hand stretched out towards the door. It opens softly and old women begin to come in, crossing them-selves on the threshold, and kneeling down in front of the stage with red petticoats over their heads.

Maurya *(half in a dream, to* Cathleen*).* Is it Patch, or Michael, or what is it at all?

Cathleen. Michael is after being found in the far north, and when he is found there how could he be here in this place?

Maurya. There does be a power of young men floating round in the sea, and what way would they know if it was Michael they had, or another man like him, for when a man is nine days in the sea, and the wind blowing, it's hard set his own mother would be to say what man was in it.

Cathleen. It's Michael, God spare him, for they're after sending us a bit of his clothes from the far north.

She reaches out and hands Maurya *the clothes that belonged to Michael.* Maurya *stands up slowly, and takes them in her hands.* Nora *looks out.*

Nora. They're carrying a thing among them, and there's water dripping out of it and leaving a track by the big stones.

Cathleen *(in a whisper to the women who have come in).* Is it Bartley it is?

One of the Women. It is, surely, God rest his soul.

Two younger women come in and pull out the table. Then men carry in the body of Bartley, *laid on a plank, with a bit of a sail over it, and lay it on the table.*

Cathleen *(to the women as they are doing so).* What way was he drowned?

One of the Women. The grey pony knocked him over into the sea, and he was washed out where there is a great surf on the white rocks.

Maurya *has gone over and knelt down at the head of the table. The women are keening softly and swaying themselves with a slow movement.* Cathleen *and* Nora *kneel at the other end of the table. The men kneel near the door.*

Maurya *(raising her head and speaking as if she did not see the people around her).* They're all gone now, and there isn't anything more the sea can do to me... I'll have no call now to be up crying and praying when the wind breaks from the south and you can hear the surf is in the east, and the surf is in the west, making a great stir with the two noises, and they hitting one on the other. I'll have no call now to be going down and getting Holy Water in the dark nights after Samhain, and I won't care what way the sea is when the other women will be keening. *(To* Nora) Give me the Holy Water, Nora; there's a small sup still on the dresser.

Nora *gives it to her.*

Maurya *(drops Michael's clothes across* Bartley's *feet, and sprinkles the Holy Water over him).* It isn't that I haven't prayed for you, Bartley, to the Almighty God. It isn't that I haven't said prayers in the dark night till you wouldn't know what I'd be saying; but it's a great rest I'll have now, and it's time, surely. It's a great rest I'll have now, and great sleeping in the long nights after Samhain, if it's only a bit of wet flour we do have to eat, and maybe a fish that would be stinking.

She kneels down again, crossing herself, and saying prayers under her breath.

Cathleen *(to an old man)*. Maybe yourself and Eamon would make a coffin when the sun rises. We have fine white boards herself bought. God help her, thinking Michael would be found, and I have a new cake you can eat while you'll be working.

The Old Man *(looking at the boards)*. Are there nails with them?

Cathleen. There are not, Colum; we didn't think of the nails.

Another Man. It's a great wonder she wouldn't think of the nails, and all the coffins she's seen made already.

Cathleen. It's getting old she is, and broken.

Maurya *stands up again very slowly and spreads out the pieces of Michael's clothes beside the body, sprinkling them with the last of the Holy Water.*

Nora *(in a whisper to* Cathleen*)*. She's quiet now and easy; but the day Michael was drowned you could hear her crying out from this to the spring well. It's fonder she was of Michael, and would anyone have thought that?

Cathleen *(slowly and clearly)*. An old woman will be soon tired with anything she will do, and isn't it nine days herself is after crying and keening and making great sorrow in the house?

Maurya *(puts the empty cup mouth downwards on the table, and lays her hands together on Bartley's feet)*. They're all together this time, and the end is come. May the Almighty God have mercy on Bartley's soul, and on Michael's soul, and on the souls of Sheamus and Patch, and Stephen and Shawn *(bending her head)*; and may He have mercy on my soul, Nora, and on the soul of every one is left living in the world.

She pauses, and the keen rises a little more loudly from the women, then sinks away.

Maurya *(continuing)*. Michael has a clean burial in the far north, by the grace of the Almighty God. Bartley will have a fine coffin out of the white boards, and a deep grave surely. What more can we want than that? No man at all can be living for ever, and we must be satisfied.

She kneels down again and the curtain falls slowly.

stories of the seanchaí

seán o'sullivan

All but one of these stories were originally published in Sean O'Sullivan's *Folktales of Ireland*. Sean O'Sullivan, born in Tuosist, Co. Kerry, is recognised as one of the foremost authorities on the Irish oral tradition. These stories, which he collected in various parts of the country, are typical examples of the art of the *Seanchaí*, handed down from generation to generation by word of mouth.

In former times each rural area had its own *Seanchaí* – an old man who combined a rich store of folklore with the ability to tell a story well. His neighbours would gather nightly to listen to the tales he related as he sat at the fireside.

The following were the qualities of a good *seanchaí:* he told stories often and he loved to tell them; he had an outstanding memory and was able to master a huge body of narratives and recite them perfectly; he had a musical voice both when speaking Gaelic and English; he used few bodily movements and spoke slowly; he knew when to pause for effect (especially after an important event in the story, to allow each listener to picture the event in his imagination and savour it), and these pauses were never more than ten seconds or so; he looked at each member of the audience, then down for a time, then into the fire for a time; and, he smiled but did not laugh after telling something amusing that aroused great merriment among his listeners.

The *seanchaí* never rose from the corner of the fireplace, and if he gestured too much in attempting to act out the story he was laughed at. No interruptions were allowed once the storytelling commenced. No one asked questions. No words of encouragement or praise were given as in singing and dancing. No one dared sleep, and no one wanted to when a good narrator held forth.

Here are a selection of stories told by a seanchaí:

A NARROW ESCAPE

IT WAS ON A FINE SUNDAY NIGHT many years ago, my father sent me to call the members of his crew as he had decided to moor some fishing nets in order to get bait to enable them to shoot the long lines for heavy ground fish on the following day. It being the Sabbath day he would not set the nets until after midnight. I was only a boy at the time but as one of the crew of four failed to turn up and the night was fine, my father allowed me to take his place in the four-man curagh.

It was a bright starlit night and when the nets were moored about a mile from the shore we started to row homewards when we saw the lights of a ship coming from the open sea through the Sound. As my father was a ship's pilot we immediately raced for the approaching ship. After about half an hour's hard pulling the lights appeared to be as far away as when we first saw them, so we eased up to watch them for a few minutes. My father took his match box out and cracked several matches to attract the attention of those on board, and as if in answer to those signals the ship seemed to swing round towards us and was aglow with lights that we had not seen before. "He has seen our lights now," said one of the men and we continued to row harder than ever towards him, but although we went a considerable distance this time, it seemed to us that he was as far away as ever.

We were now several miles from our own shore and drawing closer to the towering Cliffs of Moher where there was no landing place for miles on either side, a most dangerous coast indeed and more so at night. Suddenly we noticed that it had grown darker; the sky had become overcast and a rough swell in the sea had set in. The ship's lights had grown dim and finally disappeared entirely. There was nothing to do now but to make for home so the curagh was turned about.

We had not pulled half a dozen strokes when, there off our stern, within two cables-length, lay a big ship ablaze with lights. We were all excited now and about went the curagh again as we made for the ship with all speed, but although we rowed hard for fully fifteen minutes, she appeared as far away as before.

I had noticed for some time now that my father was paying little attention to the ship but was looking at the sky and at the sea. He had been silent for some time, but now he ordered us to pull for home with all speed. The ship's lights had grown very dim again, so we headed for home. I was very disappointed as I had expected to be able to go aboard a big ship for the first time and see the foreign sailors and get some ship's biscuits and maybe a coconut and some nice souvenirs from the ship's officers.

The sea had by now got rather rough, with strong gusts of wind. After a long hard pull we got back close to the strand from where we had put off, and by that time we had almost forgotten about the ship as it required all our skill and vigilance in the darkness to avoid the short, steep lumps of sea and prevent any of them coming aboard and swamping us. As it was, we were shipping a lot of water and I was kept bailing it out as fast as it came in. Once as we rode on the crest of a wave one of the men cried out that he saw the ship lights again, but my father silenced him by saying that the sooner we could get ashore the better.

When we had got within a few hundred yards of the beach there was a lull; the wind died away and it became quite calm. One of the men remarked that it was going to be a good night after all, but my father said that there would be a sudden shift of wind at any moment and it would be worse presently. We hauled up the curragh, got it into its place and had just secured it when the shift of wind came. It came with a roar and blew right in on the beach, lashing the sea into a fury and almost taking us off our own feet.

Had we been a few minutes later in getting ashore it would have caught us. Our curragh could never have weathered the heavy seas, and we should have been swamped in trying to run for the beach. "We were very lucky to be ashore before it came," said one of the men, "we were just in time." "It was all because of that queer ship," said another. They then separated and went home.

Before going to bed I was tempted to have another look to see if the ship was in sight, and there, close in off the strand, much nearer than where our nets were moored, was a vessel with many-coloured lights. I ran and excitedly told my father, who was kneeling down beside the fire saying his rosary before going to bed. He motioned me to be silent and shut the door, after which I went to bed, and falling asleep, dreamt about ships and sailors, coconuts and ship's biscuits, panama straw hats and leather waist-bands with beautiful designs.

I awoke about daybreak and looked out. The storm had spent itself but there was still a strong breeze blowing in on the strand. After starting the fire and putting on the kettle, I went to see if any wreckage had been washed ashore. I picked up an empty tin which had contained some ship's biscuits, and further on I found a coconut cracked in two and, of course, empty.

THE CHILDREN OF THE DEAD WOMAN

THERE WAS A MAN LONG AGO, and he was looking for a wife. He found one, but he was only a year married to her when she died, while giving birth to a child. Her mother was anxious to have the child to rear, but the father said that he would not give the child away to anybody. He would try to rear it himself. At that time, there were old women who earned their living by minding children; so the father got one of them to look after his own child. The only people in the house besides the child were this old woman and himself. He was a very strong man. Two months went by. The old woman slept in a bed beside the fire with the cradle nearby, so that she was able to attend to the child by night and by day.

One stormy evening, the father came home from his work. He took off his boots and sat beside the fire.

He took up the child, saying, "You are doing well, my little orphan, and getting strong."

"May God give you long life," said he to the old woman. "You are minding him well, to say that he is thriving so fast!"

"You don't know what I know," replied the old woman. "Every night since she died — at least, since I came here — that child's mother comes here. She eats some boiled potatoes and drinks some milk from the cupboard. The moment she comes in, she goes over to the cradle and kisses the child. Then she warms her hands at the fire before taking the boiled potatoes and milk from the cupboard. When she has taken some food, she comes to the cradle again, takes up the child, and feeds him at her breast. Then she washes him, puts dry clothes under him and lays him down in the cradle, kissing him. She then stands in the middle of the floor, looks up toward the room, where you are asleep, heaves a sigh, and goes out the door. She has done that every night since I came here. I see her, but I don't ask her any question."

"Had I known that," said the man, "and had I seen her, I would have held her here or failed in the attempt."

"You'll get your chance," said the old woman. "I will cough tonight when she comes. Have your ears open."

That night he did not take off all of his clothes but lay on the bed, so that he would see her when she came and hold her.

Late that night, they heard the door opening. She came in and kissed the child; then she went to the cupboard, got the dish of potatoes and the naggin of milk – naggins were common vessels at that time – and ate quickly. She then stirred up the fire and warmed herself. (I'd say she was cold). When she had warmed herself, she went to the cradle, took up the child, suckled him, washed and cleaned him, and put dry clothes under him. Then she stood in the middle of the floor and looked up toward the room. The old woman coughed, and the woman went out the door.

"Are you awake now?" asked the old woman.

"I am," replied the man, coming down from the room.

"Did you see her?"

"I did, but I was too frightened to go near her. And I thought that if I saw her at all, I'd hold her here."

The two of them did not go to bed until it dawned. The man went next morning to the house of his wife's parents. Her three brothers were there, two of them were strong, hefty fellows, but the third was a weakling. The family welcomed him and asked him how the child was doing. He told them the child was thriving, that his mother came each night to wash and clean and suckle him.

"I saw her myself last night," said he. "She ate some potatoes and drank milk after attending to the child. Then she went out the door, and I was too frightened to move."

"Bad luck to you," said the eldest brother. "If you saw her, you could have held her. If I were there, I'd not let her go."

"Well, come over to me tonight then, and you'll see her," said the husband. "We'll see if you can hold her."

"If I see her, I'll hold her," said the brother.

They walked back to the house again. The old woman and the child were there. When they sat down, the dead woman's brother asked the old woman did his sister come every night. She said that she did.

"Well, if I see her tonight, I won't let her go," said he.

Early in the night, the dead woman's husband and brother went up to the bedroom and kept watch to see if she would come. It wasn't long until they heard the door opening. Her brother saw her as well as the husband and the old woman. She went up to the fire and warmed her hands. (I suppose she was always cold). When she had warmed herself, she went to the cupboard, took out the dish of potatoes and a naggin of milk and ate quickly. Then she went to the cradle, took up the child, and put him to her breast. She cleaned and washed him and put dry clothes under him. Then she stood in the middle of the floor, looked up toward the room, heaved a sigh, and went out.

"Are ye asleep?" asked the old woman.

"No," they replied, as they came down from the room.

"Ye are the two most cowardly men I've ever met," said the old woman.

(I must shorten my story for you now). The same thing happened to the second brother.

"May the devil take ye!" said the third brother. "If I were there, I'd hold her."

"Bad cess to you! You're able to do nothing," replied the two brothers.

"I'll tell ye what I can do," said the youngest brother. "If I saw my sister, I'd hold her and wouldn't let her go. If ye come along with me tonight, ye'll see that I'll hold her if I lay eyes on her."

The three brothers went to the house that night. Before it was too late, they decided to go up to the bedroom. They lay down, the youngest on the outside, so that he could easily run down to the kitchen to catch his sister. It wasn't long until they heard the door opening, and in she came. They all saw her. She ran to the fire and warmed her hands. Then she went to the cupboard and took out the potatoes and milk. She seemed to be very hungry. After eating, she sat down and took the child from the cradle and put him to her breast; then she washed and cleaned him and put dry clothes under and about him.

As she put him back into the cradle, she kissed him three times. On the other nights, she had kissed him only once. She then stood up to leave. Weren't the four men great cowards that they made no move? Just then, up jumped the youngest brother, and he put his two arms around her. She screamed and begged him, for God's sake, to let her go. In the struggle, she lifted him up to the rafters, beseeching him to release her.

"I'll be killed if I'm not back in time," she cried.

"The devil a foot will you put out of here," said her brother.

She was dragging him about, almost killing him; so he shouted to one of his brothers to come to his assistance. The pair of them struggled with her until she finally fell down on the floor in a dead faint. The youngest brother still kept his hold of her.

Next morning, her husband went with one of the brothers for the priest. When they came back, the priest prayed over her until ten o'clock, while her young brother held her. When she recovered her speech, she told the priest that that was to have been her last visit, as the fairies with whom she stayed were moving to Ulster that night. So she stayed with her husband and child, much the same as she had been before, except that she had a wild look in her eyes till the day she died. She bore nine sons to her husband after her rescue, and they came to be known as the children of the dead woman.

THE COW THAT ATE THE PIPER

THERE WERE THREE SPALPEENS coming home to Kerry from Limerick one time after working there. On their way, they met a piper on the road.

"I'll go along with ye," said the piper.

"All right," they said.

The night was very cold, freezing hard, and they were going to perish. They saw a dead man on the road with a new pair of shoes on his feet.

"By heavens!" said the piper, "I haven't a stitch of shoes on me. Give me that spade to see can I cut off his legs."

"Twas the only way he could take off the shoes. They were held on by the frost. So he took hold of the spade and cut off the two feet at the ankles. He took them along with him. They got lodgings at a house where three cows were tied in the kitchen.

"Keep away from that gray cow," said the servant girl, "or she'll eat your coats. Keep out from her."

They all went to sleep. The three spalpeens and the piper stretched down near the fire. The piper heated the shoes and the dead man's feet at the fire and got the shoes off. He put on the shoes and threw the feet near the gray cow's head. Early next morning, he left the house wearing his new pair of shoes. When the servant girl got up, she looked at the door. It was bolted, and the three spalpeens were asleep near the fire.

"My God!" she cried. "There were four of ye last night, and now there are only three. Where did the other man go?"

"We don't know," they said. "How would we know where he went?"

She went to the gray cow's head and found the two feet.

"Oh my!" she cried. "He was eaten by her."

She called the man of the house.

"The gray cow has eaten one of the men," said she.

"What's that you're saying?" said the farmer.

"I'm telling the truth," said she. "There's only his feet left. The rest of him is eaten."

The farmer got up. "There were four of ye there last night, men," said he.

"There were," said one of the spalpeens, "and our comrade has been eaten by the cow."

"Don't cause any trouble about it," said the farmer. "Here's five pounds for ye. Eat your breakfast and be off. Don't say a word."

They left when they had the breakfast eaten. And they met the piper some distance from the house, and he dancing on the road. Such a thing could happen!

THE MARCH COCK AND THE COFFIN

THERE WAS A HOUSE IN THIS TOWNLAND, in which I am telling my story, and a man lived there with his wife and children. The man worked every day not far from the house, and whenever he looked toward the house, he would see a coffin descending from the sky on the side of the house. At the same moment each day, the March cock, which was in the house, used to jump up, shake his wings, and crow loudly. Then he used to try to fly up on the gable, and if he couldn't do that, he would settle on the chimney and keep crowing until he banished the coffin.

That went on for three weeks or so, and the man saw it happening each day. The woman of the house came to hate the cock on account of its crowing. Then one day, when the man was in the field, he saw the coffin coming down on the side of the house. The cock was inside in the house and he jumped up, shook his wings, and started to crow. The woman was so annoyed that she took up a wooden mallet and threw it at the cock to drive him from the house, so that she wouldn't be listening to him. She hit the cock on the head and killed him with the blow. The coffin remained where it was. The man was worried and he went to the house and found the cock dead.

"Who killed the cock?" he asked.

"I did," said his wife. "My head was split from his crowing day after day. I threw the mallet at him to drive him away, but I struck him on the head and killed him."

"My seven thousand curses on you!" said the husband. "You killed the cock and you killed me too!"

He lay down on the bed, and in three days' time, he was dead.

That's as true a story as was ever told. It happened here in this townland, and the house where the man and the cock were can still be seen by anybody.

The dear blessing of God and of the Church on the souls of the dead! And may we be seventeen hundred thousand times better off a year from tonight — ourselves and all who are listening to me.

THE UGLIER FOOT

THERE WAS A TAILOR IN BALLYVOURNEY a long time ago. He had very big ankles, and the nickname the people had on him was Tadhg of the Ankles. At that time, tradesmen travelled from house to house, and the people used to gather up for sport and fun with them.

One night Tadhg was sewing away, sitting on the table, and he had one of his legs stretched out from him. The woman of the house was sitting at the head of the table, between Tadhg and the fire. She noticed Tadhg's big ankle.

"Upon my conscience, that's an ugly foot," said she. One or two people laughed at this.

"Upon my conscience," said Tadhg, "there's a still uglier foot than it in the house."

The woman of the house must have had badly shaped feet herself, and she thought that Tadhg was hinting at her.

"There isn't an uglier foot than it in the whole world," said she.

"Would you lay a bet on that?" asked Tadhg.

"I would," said she.

"I'll bet you a quart of whiskey that there's an uglier foot than it in this house," said Tadhg.

"I'll take the bet," said the woman.

At that, Tadhg pulled his other foot from under him.

"Now," said he, "which is the uglier, the first foot or the second one?"

"Upon my word, the second is a lot uglier," said the woman.

"Very well," said Tadhg. "Send out for a quart of whiskey for me."

"I will, indeed," said the woman.

She was glad to have lost the bet when her own feet weren't compared to Tadhg's.

THE FOX AND THE EAGLE

THERE CAME A VERY BAD YEAR one time. One day the fox was near the shore of the Lakes of Killarney, and he couldn't find a bird or anything else to eat. Then he spied three ducks a bit out from the shore and thought to himself that if he could catch hold of them, he would have a fine meal. There was some water parsnip with very large leaves growing by the shore, and he swam out to it and cut off two big leaves of it with his teeth. He held one of them at each side of his mouth and swam towards the ducks. They never felt anything until he had taken one of them off with him.

Very satisfied with himself, he brought her ashore, laid her down, and decided to try and catch the other two as well — 'tis seldom they would be on offer!

He caught a second duck by the same trick and left her dead near the first. Then out he swam for the third and brought her in. But, if he did, there was no trace of the other two where he had left them.

"May God help me!" said he. "I have only the one by my day's work. What'll I do? I wonder who is playing tricks on me."

He looked all around but couldn't see an enemy anywhere. Then he looked towards the cliff that was nearby, and what did he spy but the nest of an eagle high up on it.

"No one ever took my two ducks but the eagle," said he. "As good as I am at thieving, there's a bigger thief above my head."

He didn't know how to get at the eagle. Then he saw a fire smouldering not far away, where men had been working at a quarry a few days before. They had a fire and it was still burning slowly under the surface of the ground. He dragged the duck to the fire and pulled her hither and thither through the embers. Then he left her down on the grass and hid. The eagle must have been watching out for the third duck too, for down he swooped and snatched her up to his nest. No sooner did the dead duck's body touch the dry nest than the nest caught fire — there were live embers stuck in the duck's feathers. Down fell the blazing nest with the three dead ducks as well as the eagle's three young ones inside it, so the fox had six birds for his supper. Didn't he get his own back well on the eagle?

ACKNOWLEDGEMENTS

We would like to thank Ann Jackson and Brian Kavanagh for work in the development of the materials; Tim O'Neill for reading and commenting on the manuscript; Mr. Seamus Heaney for 'The Evening Land', 'Inisheer' and 'The Oarsman's Song'; A. D. Peters and Co. Ltd. for extracts from *Famine* by Liam O'Flaherty; for extracts from *The Islanders* by Tomas O'Crohan, by permission of the Oxford University Press; Dr. Brendan Kennelly for 'Sea'; for 'Years Later' from 'The Cleggan Disaster' reprinted by permission of Faber and Faber Ltd. from *Sailing to an Island* by Richard Murphy; for 'The Thatcher' reprinted by permission of Faber and Faber Ltd. from *Door into the Dark* by Seamus Heaney; Wolfhound Press for 'The Test of Courage' from *The Pedlar's Revenge and Other Stories* (1976) by Liam O'Flaherty; Jonathan Cape Ltd., for 'Spring Sowing', 'The Letter' and 'Going into Exile' from *The Short Stories of Liam O'Flaherty;* Mrs. Kate Mulkerrins and Chatto and Windus for 'A Day's Hunting' from Maurice O'Sullivan's *Twenty Years A-Growing;* the University of Chicago Press and Sean O'Sullivan for 'The Children of the Dead Woman', 'The Cow that ate the Piper', 'The March Cock and the Coffin', 'The Uglier Foot' and 'The Fox and the Eagle' from *Folk Tales of Ireland.*

In instances where we have failed to trace the copyright holder, we would be grateful if they would contact the publisher.

We would like to thank the following for permission to reproduce photographs: Pat Langan and *The Irish Times* pages 2 and 3, 6, 10, 18 bottom, 23, 24, 34, 48, 61, 65, 76, 80, 95, 98 bottom, 100, 113, 117, 119, 121, 133, 137, 149, 153, 159, 161, 168, 172, 179, 190, 197, 214, 226, 237. Bord Failte Eireann pages 18 top, 27, 30, 41 top, 20, 47, 67, 70, 85, 87, 93, 98 top, 129 bottom, 157, 162, 184; The Director of the National Museum of Ireland pages 24, 37, 41 bottom, 42, 52, 55, 60, 129 top, The Director of the National Library of Ireland pages 106, 107, 111, 141, 145, 203.